Leonard Thompson

Card in back

A GALAXY OF SAINTS

A GALAXY OF
SAINTS

Lesser-Known Bible Men and Women

HERBERT F. STEVENSON

FOREWORD BY
PAUL S. REES

FLEMING H. REVELL COMPANY

Foreword

The reversed judgments of history are part of its fascination. If in time's lengthened perspective some large figures are ensmalled, it is beyond denying that some small figures are enlarged.

It was a lovely summer's day, not long ago, when I motored with friends from Glasgow in Scotland to Keswick in England. Among the towns through which we passed was Ecclefechan, home of rugged old Carlyle. Well, there's the story of the day they brought his body back to this little border town for burial. The historian Froude, so it is reported, rushed up to the station-master and said anxiously: "I hope every precaution is being taken to prevent unseemly crowding; that the police have taken proper measures to ensure the road being kept clear between the station and the churchyard."

"Eh, man," was the reply, "ye needna fash yersel. There's nae an auld wife in Ecclefechan that wud put her heed oot o' the window tae look at Tam Carlyle when he was leevin', let alane when he's deed!"

If his contemporaries "wrote him off" as unimportant, posterity has indubitably reversed their judgment. In this phenomenon may be found, in part, the significance of the chapters that follow. In a quiet, exploratory, revealing way, the author has shown us something of the worth and glory of Bible characters who, denied much in the way of *space* in the inspired record, are nevertheless to be credited with much in the way of *grace*.

I have just used the phrase "in part." Let me explain. There are some figures that obviously had a high rating in the minds of their contemporaries, yet have tended to fade out simply because we, reading the record long afterward, have not assessed their worth as generously as the record warrants. Mr. Stevenson's essays greatly help to restore the balance.

You will linger a bit, I hope, over the final chapter. Here you come upon fame without name. Here is where admiration salutes the anonymous. One day the muses pointed their golden wands at a non-conformist, and he wrote:

> One feast of holy days the crest,
>   I though no churchman love to keep;
> "All saints," the unknown good that rest,
>   In God's still memory, folded deep!
> The bravely dumb that did their deed,
>   And scorned to blot it with a name:
> Men of the plain, heroic breed,
>   That loved Heaven's silence more than fame.

They are in this closing chapter—and the length of the list will surprise you.

And now, please, read! You will be the better for it!

PAUL S. REES

Introduction

It is one of the many paradoxes of the Bible that its divine inspiration is attested most convincingly by the fact that it is so *human*. The "scriptures" of other world religions usually contain undiluted dogma and doctrine: the Bible is largely taken up with the experiences of men and women to whom the Word of God came. It tells of the reactions of ordinary people to the divine self-revelation: the effect upon them of faith in God, on the one hand, or disregard of His law, on the other. Men and women, youths and maidens are represented in the Bible stories: great men, and the insignificant—the whole range of human personality.

Much has been written about the outstanding Biblical characters; but thrilling and inspiring stories abound of more humble folk—the "lesser lights" who throughout the centuries have been the torch-bearers of the faith. In his gallery of heroes the writer of the epistle to the Hebrews refers, at the close of chapter eleven, to the great number of whom time would fail to tell, who "wrought righteousness, obtained promises... of whom the world was not worthy." Some of these inheritors of the promises —and their New Testament successors—rendered outstanding service to their day and generation, and became examples of faith for all time. Ordinary people, they have more than ordinary interest for the ordinary folk who "follow in their train." If *they* endured and accomplished so much, then so can we! And they inspire us with a lofty conception of our high calling in Christ. For the vitality of the work and witness of the Church is maintained—much as it owes to its leaders— by the rank and file.

It is hoped that these studies in the lives of some such will aid toward the realization of the aspiration—"wherefore seeing we also are compassed about with so great a cloud of witnesses, let us lay aside every weight, and the sin which doth so easily beset, and let us run with patience the race that is set before us, looking unto Jesus. . . ."

I would express my gratitude to Dr. Paul Rees, who for the second time has rendered me the inestimable encouragement of writing a Foreword, and to Miss D. Tarrant for permission to reproduce her late father's poem "Famous Men," based upon the renowned panegyric in Ecclesiasticus 44: 1–15. Some of these studies have appeared in *The Life of Faith*, and I am grateful for the appreciation of readers who, like Oliver Twist, asked for more. Incidentally, the chapters in Part II were written twenty years ago: which explains any difference in style from the rest of the book.

Now praise we great and famous men,
    The fathers, named in story;
And praise the Lord, who now as then
    Reveals in man His glory.

Praise we the wise and brave and strong
    Who graced their generation;
Who helped the right, and fought the wrong,
    And made our folk a nation.

Praise we the great of heart and mind,
    The singers sweetly gifted,
Whose music like a mighty wind
    The souls of men uplifted.

Praise we the peaceful men of skill,
    Who builded homes of beauty,
And, rich in art, made richer still
    The brotherhood of duty.

Praise we the glorious names we know,
    And they whose names have perished—
Lost in the haze of long ago—
    In silent love be cherished.

In peace their sacred ashes rest,
    Fulfilled their day's endeavour;
They blessed the earth, and they are blessed
    Of God and man for ever.

So praise we great and famous men,
    The fathers, named in story;
And praise the Lord, who now as then
    Reveals in man His glory.

WILLIAM GEORGE TARRANT.

Contents

PART I

SOME OLD TESTAMENT "LESSER LIGHTS"

PART II

SOME OF THE LESSER-KNOWN APOSTLES

PART III

SOME NEW TESTAMENT SAINTS

PART I

SOME OLD TESTAMENT "LESSER LIGHTS"

Now all these things (i.e. the experiences recorded in the Old Testament) happened unto them for ensamples: and they are written for our admonition—1 Corinthians 10: 11.

"Human life is much the same, whether lived eighteen hundred years on this side or eighteen hundred years on that side of the Cross; whether hidden beneath our broadcloth, or the flowing robes of an Arab sheikh; whether spent in modern towns, or on the free, open pasture-lands of Southern Palestine.

"Our critics complain of our poring over these time-worn pages of ancient biography; but, with all deference to them, we feel bound to say that we learn better how to live, we inhale more spiritual ozone, we see further into the reasons of God's dealings with men, when doing so, than when scanning the pages of yesterday's newspaper or of a society journal."

F. B. MEYER.
Israel, A Prince with God.

1

Seth: The Pioneer of Family Worship

I N the long history of the human race, no story is more tragic
than that of the opening chapter. Two words sum up that
tragedy—Paradise lost. Eloquent as these words are, however, we can never fully apprehend all that they convey, for
we have no conception of the glory and blessedness of Eden:
two people only enjoyed the great privilege of inhabiting that
earthly paradise, and they marred it through sin and were
driven hence by the flaming sword of avenging cherubim.
Adam fell, and sin and death began their age-long reign.

Swiftly the dread story proceeds, to the lifting up of the
murderous hand of Cain against his brother Abel. What
bitterness must have filled the hearts of Adam and Eve as by
that one stroke they lost both their sons: the younger slain by
his brother, and that brother banished and worse than dead to
them. "Sin, when it is finished, bringeth forth death" (Jas.
1: 15); and it did not take long to do so in its most hideous
manifestation. Adam and Eve saw indeed the terrible fruit
of their wanton sowing. Perhaps their most poignant sorrow
lay in the dashing of their hopes concerning these lads; for in
addition to the normal yearnings and aspirations of all parents
for their sons, they cherished the promise of God to Eve that
her seed should bruise the serpent's head. Of course they little
realized the full meaning of that pledge, and looked for an
immediate fulfilment in their sons. Now one was dead and the
other a fratricide! One had been slain despite—nay, because of
—an acceptable act of worship; the other had committed
murder in an outburst of long-suppressed jealousy.

It seemed like the end of all their hopes and expectations:

as if the very promise of God had proved a falsehood. Then, in that darkest hour, God—as He so often delights to do— amazed and delighted them with a new manifestation of His faithfulness and grace. He gave them another son, in place of Abel; and Eve "called his name Seth [*i.e.* 'appointed']; for God, said she, hath appointed me another seed instead of Abel whom Cain slew" (Gen. 4: 25).

Disastrously as the course of evil had proceeded, now its terrible consequences are countered as the story of God's intervening grace unfolds: "And to Seth, to him also there was born a son; and he called his name Enos: *then began men to call upon the name of the Lord*" (v. 26). We know nothing more of Seth than that—except that he "begat sons and daughters" and lived to be nine hundred and twelve years old (5: 7, 8). So brief a biography; yet how revealing is the one significant sentence concerning him! During his time, in his family, men "*began to call upon the name of the Lord.*" What an epitaph for a son of Adam and brother of Cain!

The brevity of the comment upon him, however, tends to obscure its vast import; and amid the enthralling stories more fully told in Genesis, that of Seth is apt to be overlooked. Indeed, he is often hidden behind his posterity, in some such phrase as "the godly line of Seth"—as if he, the progenitor, were worthy of remembrance for that fact only! But he was a notable character in his own right, in the age-long drama of redemption. For of his seed came Christ, according to the flesh; and in his day men began to call upon the name of the Lord. Beginnings are always interesting and important: how supremely so is the story of man's beginning to call upon the name of the Lord!

Various suggestions have been made as to what that phrase precisely means. Some commentators support the marginal rendering, "then men began to call themselves by the name of Jehovah," and say that it means that the significance of the sacred name first began to be realized; while others opine that then the true worshippers were called "Jehovah-worshippers" by the ungodly, perhaps in scorn. But these views do not satisfy the sense of crisis and vital significance aroused by the statement. Nor do the majority of scholars adopt that alternative rendering: most translators and commentators adhere to the text of the Authorized Version. Now the phrase, "to call upon the name of the Lord," occurs frequently in Scripture, and uniformly means the drawing near to God in worship, through the appointed means of sacrifice. It seems most convincing, therefore, as well as most natural, to interpret this verse as signifying that in the household of Seth, following the birth of Enos, the worship of God first became a vital and ordered part of individual and family life.

The story of Cain and Abel reveals that sacrifices had been offered by them—but obviously as something occasional and unusual. As a consequence of the fall, Adam and Eve had forfeited the fellowship with God they enjoyed in Eden, and seemingly were unable to adjust themselves to a different kind of relationship upon the basis of sacrifice. The manifest uncertainty of their sons in the whole matter and manner of approach to God bears witness to the lack of regular family worship in their upbringing. It was not until Seth had established a family life of his own, after the birth of his son Enos, that "men began to call on the name of the Lord"—and undoubtedly the credit for that belongs to him: the wording of the verse clearly carries that implication. As Enoch, a few generations later, "walked with God" after begetting his son Methuselah (5: 22), so now did Seth "call upon the name of the Lord" on the birth of Enos.

Now, it is never easy to take the initiative in matters of religion. Training and habit incline us to conform to the practices in which we are reared. Moreover, to these factors, in the case of Seth, was added the lack of truly godly example. His parents were at best apathetic; his brother an outcast. Both heredity and environment were against him. Yet he became a man of God—for that is implied in "calling upon the name of the Lord." How easy it is to be a Christian in a godly home, or in an assembly of zealous believers! What a different matter it is to love and serve the Lord amid the heedless and the hostile. Seth was the pioneer of all such: he merits both our commendation and our emulation.

The effects of Seth's godly life and practices are incalculable. First, toward his parents. We are told that Adam lived a further eight hundred years after he begat Seth—that is, some seven hundred years after men "began to call upon the name of the Lord" (4: 25; 5: 4–7). Who can doubt that Adam learned from his son how to draw nigh to God: that the man through whom sin entered into the world found grace and mercy at the altar erected by his son? Eve saw something of the fulfilment of the divine promise in this son "appointed instead of Abel." We now deem it the highest privilege of parents to lead their children into the knowledge of God, and to train them in ways of worship; but Adam and Eve had instead given their sons a terrible heritage of bondage to sin and death. They, who had sinned in Eden, when in the very image and likeness of God, probably felt themselves unqualified in their fallen state to speak of godliness to their offspring. But God stepped in, and reversed the natural order of events: and the son He had given them led the parents into a new knowledge of God, and renewed faith in Him. Can we not indulge the conviction that joy once more entered their lives and home, and peace that passeth all understanding, as they "called upon the name of the Lord"?

Nowadays, alas, the majority of young people are brought up without instruction and example in godliness in their homes; and when, by the grace of God, such are led to a knowledge of the Lord Jesus Christ as their Saviour, it is often by no means easy to worship and witness there. But it is in the home that faith in Christ should find its truest expression —irrespective of whether parents and families are sympathetic, indifferent, or hostile. Many who have, haltingly and in some fear, yet in simple faith "called upon the name of the Lord" in their homes, have had the joy of leading the stumbling feet of their parents—who should have led *them*—to the Cross. Some, like Seth, have parents who enjoyed fellowship with God long ago, but have forfeited it through neglect and sin. How happy a privilege is their children's to lead them back again into a relationship of faith and love toward God! Whether this be so or not, all who worship and witness in their homes, whatever the seeming result, are accomplishing more than they can ever estimate or assess: for a godly life is a "sweet savour unto God" which, like the fragrance of Mary of Bethany's ointment, fills the house.

Not only his parents, but also the posterity of Seth were benefited by his faith and godliness—"then *began* men to call upon the name of the Lord." He established the practice of worship which has been the greatest factor for good in all subsequent history. We can never measure the influence of simple faith in God, and the expression of love toward Him. As the full-flowing river traces its source to the spring among the mountains, so all true praise and prayer, through all the generations, derive their inspiration from the regular, ordered worship of the family of Seth.

Finally, the significance of the "family altar"—family worship, led by the family's head—cannot be over-emphasized. Thus "began men to call upon the name of the Lord," and thus He would have them proceed. We have our churches, and other means of communal worship, fellowship and witness—and rightly, scripturally so; but the centre and testing-place of religion is the home. There, Adam and Eve failed—with such disastrous effects. There, Seth "broke the entail" of sin's havoc, and began to call upon the name of the Lord. There we all should live and worship and witness as His children—His redeemed; upon whose name we may call, and whose name is now called upon us!

2

Sarah: A Heroine of Faith

WHILE admiring the writings of Dr. Alexander Whyte, it is impossible to accept his estimate of Sarah. His study of her, in *Bible Characters*, is a caricature which does a grave injustice to one of the noblest women of whom we have record. He has not a good word for her, but contrasts her most unfavourably with Hagar, whom he extols at her expense. Sarah "bribed" Hagar to leave Egypt, he alleges, with promises to be a mother and friend to her; she betrayed this trust, cruelly made the girl a tool, and then cast her out. In spite of this "terrible" treatment at the hands of Sarah, Dr. Whyte affirms, "Hagar, to me, stands among God's very electest saints." With all of which I strongly disagree. Sarah, indeed, has received far less than justice from the Church as a whole, as well as from Dr. Whyte in particular. Countless sermons are preached on Abraham, but how few about Sarah! Yet she is given a place, in her own right, among the heroes of faith in Hebrews 11—and she is worthy of that imperishable honour.

It is true that we know little about her except as the wife and companion of Abraham. She was his half-sister (or niece, as some think), ten years younger than he; and so beautiful that both Pharaoh of Egypt and Abimelech, king of Gerah— deceived into thinking that she was but Abraham's sister— wanted to marry her. She had so much, in her good looks and her happy marriage, that other women might envy: yet she endured a more grievous sorrow and testing than most.

When the call of God came to Abraham in Ur of the Chaldees, she, with him, left home and country to become a stranger and pilgrim in a foreign land. The whole spirit of the Scripture narrative implies that she fully entered into Abraham's vision and pilgrimage. She did not just go because she had to, as Abraham's wife: she was the true companion of his new life of obedience to, and fellowship with, God—unlike Terah and Lot, who merely kept him company for the sake of family relationship.

What she thought of the long halt at Haran, and of Abraham's lapses of faith which put her in such jeopardy, we do not know; but through all the long years of testing she is presented as Abraham's true helpmeet, learning with him lessons of faith and endurance, comforting and strengthening him in his trials. In many respects, the testing of her faith was more severe even than his. We must remember that Abraham's faith had been kindled, and was sustained, by visitations from God Himself. Sarah did not share in these; she had no personal dealings with God; she had only the testimony of Abraham. Again, the separation of Lot from Abraham would affect her more than her husband, for he had much to occupy him in the management of his large household; but she was left without womanly companionship, except that of servants, now that Lot's wife and daughters were gone.

Severest testing of all, however, lay in the fact which constituted a blight upon all her life, robbing her of joy and eventually stifling even hope—the fact expressed in Scripture with characteristic brevity in the words, "but Sarah was barren." This was the greatest sorrow and the severest reproach any wife of that day could experience: but for Sarah it was enhanced by the fact that it seemed to frustrate the divine promise to Abraham. Their entire manner of life, as pilgrims in a strange land, was established upon a promise of God—and her barrenness seemed to stand in the way of the fulfilment of her husband's cherished dreams, and even of the divine purposes.

As she heard from Abraham of the promise, and its repeated

reaffirmation, she shared with him the confidence that ultimately it would be fulfilled: but the waiting time was difficult to understand, and still more difficult to endure. It is not surprising that at length her faith failed. She loved her husband, and sorrowed to see his eager anticipation giving way to despair. It was no fierce "suicidal pride"—as Whyte avers—but an act of supreme self-effacement on the part of Sarah, which prompted her to suggest that he should have a son by Hagar. For his sake, and for the sake of the divine purposes, she submitted to this humiliation, this setting aside of her cherished longings, this exaltation of her handmaid to a privilege which would cause the servant to despise her mistress to the end of her days, and make the child of that servant—as she then thought—the heir of her husband.

She was wrong, of course: it was a lapse of faith on her part, but one which shows Sarah the woman in most kindly light.

Why did God allow her to endure this test? She had to learn, with Abraham, that although fruitfulness is eminently desirable, and is promised by God, and essential to the fulfilling of His purposes, yet there is something even more vital and precious. It is *faith*, and the close, intimate fellowship with God which is the result of long-tried faith. This is, above all things, what God desires. It was for this that ultimately He sent His Son—to obtain *a people for Himself*. Sarah had to learn that a Hagar can produce sons, but only Sarah can bear Isaac, the son of promise. For the fruitfulness He has promised can issue only out of a tried and proven faith.

So, after a further confirmation by God of His word, Abraham and Sarah were renewed in faith, and continued steadfast through long years, until at last the fulfilment became humanly impossible; and with the dying of her womb, faith died in Sarah. Then God drew near once more, in human likeness, and confirmed yet again His promise—and Sarah, listening behind the curtain of the tent, laughed. It was the bitter laugh of blighted hope and utter incredulity. At that laugh, God spake words which pierced her heart—"Is anything too hard for the

Lord?" For the first time in her life, Sarah received the challenge to faith at first-hand from God Himself. Covered in confusion, she tried to explain away her laughter of unbelief, but was again rebuked.

In that personal encounter with God, faith was quickened anew in Sarah, in whom it had died: but quite a different faith from that she had known heretofore. She had been a sharer in Abraham's faith; she had believed the promise of God to him: now she had a personal faith, begotten in her heart by the very word of God Himself. "Through faith also," we read in Hebrews 11: 11, "Sara herself received strength to conceive seed, and was delivered of a child when she was past age, because she judged Him faithful who had promised." So Isaac was born, the son of the faith of Abraham and of Sarah.

Afterward we read no more of Sarah until her death in Kirjath-arba, at the age of 127. I am convinced she did not share Abraham's final testing when he was called to offer up Isaac on Mount Moriah: for her, left at home, to know what was to transpire—without knowing of God's intervention: that would have been too much for her mother's heart to endure. Nor do I think that Abraham and Isaac told her afterward: it was a secret they shared together with God.

Sarah is the only woman in the Bible whose age at the time of death is given; surely the reason is that we might know she had thirty-seven years of happy enjoyment of her son: a long sunlit eventide, in the rest and fruitfulness of faith. God is gracious to those whose faith He tries, and rewards them abundantly.

Her long life has these lessons for us—that faith is the first essential of true godliness, and the pre-requisite of spiritual fruitfulness. Such faith comes from first-hand dealings with God. No matter how much we may be inspired and encouraged by other people, God alone can quicken the faith which truly lays hold upon the promises, and brings them to fulfilment. And finally, the story reveals the patience and kindness of God in His dealings with His wayward people. Despite her lapses of faith, He did not cast Sarah aside, but gently chided and challenged her until at length faith rested in Himself alone; and He proved Himself to be indeed the God of the impossible, whose word cannot fail.

3

Leah : The Problem of Life's Inequalities

THE manifest inequalities of life are among the greatest perplexities of the inquiring mind, and the greatest testings to faith in the divine providence. This problem is exemplified in the story of Leah and Rachel. Two sisters, enjoying the self-same heredity and environment, yet one plain and unattractive (summed up in the phrase "Leah had weak eyes"—so misleadingly translated "Leah was tender eyed" in the A.V., Gen. 29: 17), while the other was gay and pretty. Therein lay the tragedy of Leah: the elder sister, she had a physical disability which would probably have destined her— but for the treacherous ruse her father Laban and she played on Jacob—like myriads of Leahs through all the centuries since, to life-long spinsterhood. And despite her stratagem, frustration and bitterness dogged her still, in even more poignant form, as an unloved wife. We seldom gain by guile what we fail to win honourably. Treachery has a boomerang effect: as Jacob the deceiver also discovered when he was himself deceived.

This physical distinction between the two sisters may seem to some a comparatively unimportant matter: but they did not regard it so. A great gulf between them is depicted in the terse comment of Holy Writ: "Leah had weak eyes: but Rachel was beautiful and well favoured." Oh, the inexpressible heartache occasioned by unloveliness of figure or features, and the un-loved condition in which they so often result—to say nothing of the still greater deprivations and disabilities which so many have to endure. Why should some have so much of physical attractiveness, health or wealth, while others have so little? For those lavishly endowed by nature receive yet more, while the deprived are still further denied. The lovely have love lavished upon them, with all that love can bestow; while the unattractive must struggle along in loneliness as best they can.

It was perfectly natural that Jacob should fall in love with Rachel; and his wooing of her is one of the most charming stories of the Old Testament. No flight of imagination is needed, however, to realize the bitterness of heart experienced by Leah at her handsome young sister's triumph in winning the affection of their cousin. The seven years which passed so swiftly for them in the enjoyment of their courtship, were full of frustration and foreboding for her: their mutual happiness emphasized her desolation. And so the despicable trick was devised between Leah and her father, and perpetrated on what Jacob thought to be his wedding day with Rachel. Under cover of the heavy veils worn on such an occasion, Leah was wedded to Jacob instead of Rachel, and he did not realize the wicked deception until the marriage was effected. (How they managed to keep Rachel quiet one cannot imagine!) The evil was not undone but deepened by the excuse of Laban that it would violate the custom of the country for the younger daughter to be married before the elder (he had had seven years to explain that, but had not done so), and his suggestion that Jacob should marry Rachel also. Now, Abraham and Isaac, Jacob's grandfather and father, those men of faith to whom God had given great and precious promises, had been strictly monogamous; and Jacob's departure from that standard, although not explicitly condemned in Scripture, carries its own condemnation in the sad story of the bitter rivalry and hatred between the two sisters; for these evils are the inevitable accompaniments of polygamy.

Despite the great wrong of which Leah was guilty, God had compassion upon her: "when the Lord saw that Leah was hated," we read, "He opened her womb" (Gen. 29: 31). To have sons was the dearest wish of every head of a household in those days; and to present sons to their husbands the great joy and pride of wives. To Leah, the birth of Reuben brought even m ore: the hope that now Jacob would esteem and love her. She expressed this wistful longing in the name she gave her firstborn, for "Reuben" means "Behold, a son!": "for she said, Surely the Lord hath looked on my affliction; now therefore will my husband love me." But her hope was vain; and her grievous disappointment—mingled still with hope—is reflected in the name of her second son, Simeon, "Hearing," so named "Because the Lord hath heard that I was hated, He hath therefore given me this son also." Hope dies hard in the human heart, and was uppermost again in Leah's when her third son arrived: "Now this time," she said, "will my husband be joined unto me, because I have borne him three sons: therefore was his name called Levi ('Joined')." At long last, however, she faced the fact that Jacob's love was not thus to be won; and now a significant change took place in her. If we may judge by the very different kind of name she gave her fourth son, her thoughts and aspirations were no longer centred upon Jacob. She turned instead to God, who had been compassionate whereas he was cold; gracious while he was unrelenting. This time she said, "Now will I praise the Lord," and the child was named Judah, "Praise."

Now that touches the very heart of the matter. If indeed Leah found comfort and consolation in God—and we must not presume too much from a simple phrase—then she turned to the one true and unfailing source of satisfaction. With Him is none of the fickleness of men; none of the varying emotions and moods which mar human relationships: God is love, and all who draw nigh to Him find Him to be, as Paul declared, "the God of all comfort." The very disabilities and deprivations which frustrate the satisfaction of natural hopes and longings are "blessings in disguise" if they lead to a deeper trust in Him: "for all things work together for good to them that love God." This is no mere sop to the stricken heart: it is the profoundest truth concerning eternal verities and values. To come into a relationship with God of intimate fellowship and simple trust, is the supreme privilege and ultimate purpose of life; and *blessed* is every factor contributing toward it, no matter how distasteful it may for a time seem to be.

At this point the story takes another turn, for Rachel, who all her life had been envied by Leah, now in her turn "envied her sister" (30: 1), and said to Jacob, "Give me children, or else I die." So querulous, evidently, was her tone that he replied angrily, "Am I in God's stead, who hath withheld from thee the fruit of the womb?" Those who are regarded as greatly favoured are not always so contented as we might consider them to be. Certainly Rachel was not. With all her personal attractions, and the steadfast love of her husband, she wanted still more. She seems to have been essentially a worldly-minded person: the satisfactions of this life counted for everything with her. She was not content even with so large a measure of blessedness as she possessed: she must have *everything* she desired, or life wasn't worth living! Those who envy the richly endowed seldom realize how little true and abiding satisfaction they really enjoy: for the heart ever craves still more than it at present possesses—until it finds its true "home" in God.

Then follows an episode characteristic of those times and circumstances, when the two sisters pursued their rivalry by persuading Jacob to take their maids as concubines: and to both of these were born two sons. Again "God hearkened unto Leah," and she had her fifth and sixth sons, Issachar (*i.e.* "recompense") and Zebulun—whose name, "dwelling," reveals her still hankering after the love she could never hope to win: "God hath endued me with a good dowry," she exclaimed, "now will my husband dwell with me, because I have borne him six sons." Instead of winning him from Rachel, however, her "good dowry" was eclipsed by an unexpected event: "God remembered Rachel, and God hearkened unto her, and opened her womb"—and Joseph was born. What joy was hers—and what chagrin was Leah's! But even that great blessing did not suffice: in the very receiving of it Rachel grasped at more—and declared determinedly to God and to all concerned her unsatisfied desire in the very name of her child: for Joseph means "adding." "The Lord shall add to me another son" was her covetous avowal.

As thus presented in the pages of Scripture, Leah and

Rachel are not very attractive characters—though perhaps their less pleasant traits were more the product of their circumstances than of their inherent natures. However that may be, the value of the story for us is in the unfolding of the divine dealings with them. God was good to both. The unhappy situation which made them antagonists was not of God's making; yet in it He over-ruled in wondrous fairness and grace toward them both. To Leah, initially deprived, He gave sons, despite her sin; then to Rachel, after *her* experience of deprivation, He satisfied the natural yearning for a child. Through all these varied experiences God was seeking—as He is with all men—to turn their hearts unto Himself: for both experienced the goodness of God in His giving—which should have evoked their loving gratitude; and also the wooing of the Lord in His withholding. He loved both equally, as He loves all mankind; and by alternately bestowing and denying He sought to prove His grace and to quicken their trust. And Leah, whose portion held a greater share of deprivation, entered into a spiritual inheritance which her more favoured sister missed.

Rachel's strong desire was satisfied: the Lord did add to her another son: but in the bearing of him she died. One cannot but think of the words spoken long afterwards concerning Jacob's descendants, "God gave them their request, but sent leanness into their soul" (Ps. 106: 15), as applicable to Rachel also. She had said, "Give me sons, or else I die," and she had sons, but yet died. She is the archetype of those who are determined to have their own way at all costs; only to find that they lose all in obtaining their desire.

After Rachel died, Leah probably thought she would at last gain Jacob as a true husband. But did she? We can never know, for Scripture is silent on the subject. But we do read the poignant story of how, when Jacob gathered his sons around him to bless them before he died, he summed up his life-story in the one yearning sentence, "As for me, when I came from Padan, Rachel died by me in the land of Canaan in the way, and I buried her there in the way of Ephrath" (Gen. 48: 7).

Rachel was his one true love to the end: Leah never won his heart. Nevertheless, Leah's was a greater privilege. For although Rachel's elder son Joseph became so great and good a man, and in due course received from Jacob the "double portion" of the firstborn—albeit he was not strictly the firstborn—yet it was through Leah's son Judah—the one whose name marked the turning of Leah's thoughts and hopes toward God—that the Abrahamic promise was fulfilled: for our Lord was born of the tribe of Judah. And Leah was buried in the cave of Machpelah, where Abraham and Sarah lay, and Isaac and Rebekah; and where later the bones of Jacob were laid beside her (Gen. 49: 29–31). Yes, they were united in death! Never gaining his love in life, she was abidingly united with him in death; and she became also a partaker with him in the fulfilment of the divine purposes and promises.

In these considerations we are brought face to face with the real and lasting values and satisfactions of life—and not only of life, but of eternity. For the lessons of this story provide the answer to the problem of the deprivations and disabilities which so grievously overshadow the lives of so many. That answer can only be found as life is viewed in the light of eternity. The inequalities of natural gifts and graces, of place and possessions, of strength and stamina, are so seemingly unfair to the under-privileged that if this life were all then it would be impossible to believe that God is love. St. Paul frankly declares that, even in this Gospel dispensation, "If in this life only we have faith in Christ, we are of all men most pitiable" (1 Cor. 15: 19). But since life is only the prelude, the preparation for eternity, then we may well go on to say with the apostle, "I reckon that the sufferings of this present time are not worthy to be compared with the glory which shall be revealed in us" (Rom. 8: 18. Cf. 2 Cor. 4: 17, 18; 1 Pet. 1: 6, 7).

The worldly-minded despise this doctrine, and scornfully dismiss it as "pie in the sky when you die." The Communist stigmatises it as "dope for the people." But those who are taught of God find in this truth not only the explanation of seeming unfairness in the government of the universe, but also the greatest incentive to faith and hope and love. For:

> Ill that He blesses is our good,
>   And unblessed good is ill;
> And all is right that seems most wrong
>   If it be His sweet will.

4

The Daughters of Zelophehad: Who Claimed an Inheritance

IN pleasing contrast to the jealousy and mutual antagonism of Leah and Rachel is the story of the shared faith of the five daughters of Zelophehad, and their claiming and obtaining in unison a possession among the families of Israel. Their far-sighted faith not only gained an inheritance for themselves, but established a principle which marked a significant turning-point in the long struggle of women for equality of status and opportunity with men.

It was when Moses was compiling a census in preparation for the entering and apportioning of the Promised Land, that these five sisters put forward their plea (Num. 27: 1–4). Appearing before the princes and leaders of the nation, assembled judicially at the door of the tabernacle, under the presidency of Moses himself, they told how their father had died in the wilderness "in his own sin," *i.e.* in the ordinary lot of human life: he had not forfeited his right to obtain a possession in the land through any misdeed such as that of the sons of Korah (Num. 16: 1–35). He had, however, died without a male heir; but, his daughters urged, "Why should the name of our father be done away from among his family, because he hath no son? Give us therefore," they boldly requested, "a possession among the brethren of our father."

That was an unheard-of proposition! Moses, doubtless recognising the reasonable nature of the request, was neverthe-less nonplussed; for the accepted practice was that male heirs only should inherit family positions and possessions. So, wise man that he was, he submitted the problem to the Lord. Just how this was done we have no certain knowledge. The record in Scripture is terse: "Moses brought their cause before the Lord." And the divine reply was emphatic: "The daughters of Zelophehad speak right: thou shalt surely give them a possession of an inheritance among their father's brethren: and thou shalt cause the inheritance of their father to pass unto them." Moreover, this precedent became the basis of a new law: "If a man die, and have no son, then ye shall cause his inheritance to pass unto his daughter. . . ."(Num. 27:7, 8). Later was added the stipulation that, if they married, they must do so within their own tribe, or forfeit the inheritance (Num. 36: 1–12). It has been pointed out that, of all the judgments which Moses must have given during the forty years in the wilderness, these are the only two recorded in Scripture. Moreover, only through these judgments could our Lord inherit the throne of David through His mother; and by them Mary was obliged to marry within the tribe of Judah.

All this happened before Jordan was crossed or a square yard of the Promised Land possessed by the children of Israel. But these women believed the promise; they trusted in the power of God to bring that promise to pass. And their faith matched the bounty of the divine provision. There would be room enough in the land flowing with milk and honey for a full and satisfying life for them, worthy of the people of God; and they were sure that the Lord would have them enjoy it. But prevailing circumstances said no; the customs of the day and accepted canons of conduct forbad. Further, there would not be lacking those to suggest that the fact their father had died in the wilderness, without a son, was proof that God had deemed the family unworthy of a possession in the land; that His will was clear in the very facts of the case. But to none of these voices did the daughters of Zelophehad pay heed; they allowed none of these considerations to suppress the conviction of the justice of their cause, and that God would honour it. They would not be deprived of their rightful possession by the opinions and practices of others; their faith reached out to apprehend all that God was ready to give. They had a large conception of the

c

divine grace; a true perception of the heart and will of God toward them. They were pioneers of the great Gospel emancipation, whereby women are co-heirs of the promises and purposes of God. They claimed, and obtained, the promises, by faith.   By faith: for when the answer of grace came from the oracle within the tabernacle, they still had to wait long before they obtained their possession. By faith they completed the journey through the wilderness; by faith they encamped on the brink of Jordan; by faith they crossed to the other side; by faith they encompassed Jericho; by faith they tarried until the land was sufficiently subjugated for the people to settle down to normal, peaceful life. At length the time had come for the apportionment to each tribe its part of the land; and then to each family its possession within the tribal territories. And when "the lot for the tribe of Manasseh" was cast, the daughters of Zelophehad "came before Eleazar, the priest, and before Joshua the son of Nun, and before the princes, saying, The Lord commanded Moses to give us an inheritance among our brethren" (Joshua 17: 3, 4). It took courage for women to come before the most exalted personages of the nation; but these five sisters had not shrunk from pleading their cause with Moses himself, and now claimed from his successor, Joshua, the fulfilment of the promise they had then obtained. Nor were they disappointed: "therefore according to the commandment of the Lord Joshua gave them an inheritance among the brethren of their father." Faith was wondrously vindicated and richly rewarded, and they entered into their possession in the will and grace of God.

This story from so long ago enshrines principles of the spiritual life which are an abiding challenge and inspiration, not only to women, but to all the people of God. So many are kept out of the inheritance which God is ready to bestow upon all His children, because they have more regard for what is commonly said and done, and the prevailing standard of spiritual experience, than for the provision of God in Christ our Saviour. We content ourselves with what others consider to be right and proper, rather than reaching out unto the fullness of the blessing God purposes for us. But if these women had submitted to the practices of the day, they would never have possessed an inheritance in the land.

There are few with the faith and courage to lay hold upon the bounty of God. In a time of spiritual dearth, we measure ourselves by one another, and are content with a mere pittance of grace—while all spiritual blessings in heavenly places are at our disposal. Few have the spirit of Paul who, despite the quality of his life which compares with ours as that of a prince with paupers, yet declared, "Brethren, I count not myself to have apprehended . . . but I press toward the mark for the prize of the high calling of God in Christ Jesus." His great desire and determination was summed up in the words, "That I may apprehend that for which also I am apprehended of Christ Jesus."

The "inheritance" of every child of God is "the fullness of the blessing of the Gospel of Christ." But it is ours by promise; we possess it only by faith—faith which inspires the vision of "the land of far distances"; faith which dares to pierce the confines of common experience and conceptions, into the wideness of God's mercy and the measure of His willingness to impart. To us indeed are given exceeding great and precious promises; yea, all the promises of God unto His people are confirmed unto us in Christ. And the challenge comes ringing from the lips of the Lord Himself, to us as to one of old, "According to your faith be it unto you."

One further lesson we may learn from the daughters of Zelophehad. They teach us the value and strength of *corporate* faith. Many stories in the Bible, many of the "lesser lights" we are considering, emphasise the inestimable effect which the faith of one individual may have, in the history of a nation and the unfolding of the purposes of God. But, if one may chase a thousand, through strength which God supplies, then two shall put ten thousand to flight (Deut. 32: 30). It is not God's will that we should be isolated warriors in the battle; and lone pilgrims in life's journey. He has set the solitary in families, and ordained that we should be strengtheners of the faith of one another (Eph. 4: 16). Where one of these sisters might have faltered, five stood together to claim and to possess. Truly there is strength in real spiritual unity. And not only strength, but the enjoyment of the fullest privileges and blessings. For, however precious the realization of the presence of God may be when, in obedience to our Lord's command, we enter our chamber and shut the door and commune with our Father in secret, nevertheless it is to the two or three gathered together in His name that the explicit promise of the Lord is given, "there am I in the midst" (Matt. 18: 20). And it is "with all saints" that we comprehend the breadth and length and depth and height of the love of God in Christ our Lord (Eph. 3: 18).

Yes, Mahlah, Noah, Hoglah, Milcah, and Tirzar, you being dead yet speak to us, with pertinent voice, concerning spiritual possession within the compass of God's bounty!

5

Aaron: The Archetypal High Priest

SOME men are great in themselves; others, lacking such inherent qualities, nevertheless achieve greatness through their association with more dominant personalities. They are "lesser lights" maybe, but to be the companion and colleague of the truly great calls for no mean gifts of mind and character. Overshadowed by their more brilliant leaders, they yet have abilities which complement and in some instances match those of the great men they serve—and not least, a humility of mind and self-effacing loyalty which enables them to play "second fiddle." This rôle was the more difficult for Aaron, in that his superior was his younger brother—a reversal of the natural ordering, that the elder should take precedence, which demanded a good deal of grace. But it was through submission to Moses that Aaron gained exceptional opportunity, and achieved abiding greatness as Israel's first High Priest.

He lived an uneventful life until he was over eighty years of age; then, when Moses returned to Egypt to lead the children of Israel out of bondage, Aaron became his principal helper. Moses had protested to God that he was slow of speech; so God appointed Aaron to be his spokesman. Thus the association of the two brothers in their exalted tasks was established by God Himself. Whether they had known one another at all intimately in their youth, we do not know; for after his weaning Moses was brought up at the Court of Pharaoh, and probably had few if any contacts with his family—who remained in slavery. In his premature attempt to act as the deliverer of his people, at forty years of age, Moses had slain an Egyptian and been obliged to flee; and he spent the ensuing forty years as a shepherd in a remote desert region.

The two men, brothers as they were, would therefore be virtually strangers to one another when united by God in the highest offices among the people He was about to redeem from Egypt. From that time on, however, they were the most intimate co-workers together with God. Aaron became a sharer of the vision and vocation of Moses, and despite weaknesses of character and temperament proved a true co-adjutor with him through the remaining forty years of their long lives. He is an example of a man of limited capacities rising through the grace of God to heights of achievement and spiritual service which might earlier have seemed utterly impossible.

His was the part of lieutenant to Moses. And how essential is the rôle of the right-hand man! Burdens too great to be borne by one alone, no matter how gifted, can be carried when a steadfast companion is ever ready to lend a helping hand. Let us not despise Aaron as a mere "shadow" of Moses; for courage of a high order was required to withstand Pharaoh, on the part of one of that despotic monarch's slaves, albeit in the company of such an intrepid leader as Moses. No small faith was demanded, also, to cast his rod upon the ground believing that it would become a serpent, and then to grasp that writhing reptile, believing that it would become a rod again (Exod. 7: 10, 15). Aaron had plainly both a childlike and yet most manly faith in God.

Most people have the weaknesses which correspond to their good qualities; and Aaron was no exception: the spirit of submission which made him so excellent a subordinate led him sadly astray when lacking the support of the stronger will of Moses. His pusillanimous yielding to the clamour of the people for gods of gold, when Moses was in the mount with God, shows how unfitted he was for personal responsibility in the leadership of the nation. That undoubtedly is why so little is said in the Scripture by way of condemnation of Aaron for his part in this sad story: God never demands of any man more than he is well able to fulfil. He knows our frame and remembers that we are dust. And the glory of His grace is this: that He will use in His service not only a Moses, but also an Aaron.

He is portrayed to us, then, as a godly man of very ordinary gifts and somewhat weak character—so like so many of us who can make no claim to greatness, and who possess no outstanding qualities. The strong tend to despise the weak, and the gifted to look down upon the common-place: but God does not. "Ye see your calling, brethren, how that not many wise men after the flesh, not many mighty . . . are called . . ." He promises, however, that His strength shall come upon them in their weakness, so that out of weakness they shall be made strong. Thus it was with Aaron. Through fellowship with God and with His servant Moses, he at length became able to share in full measure the burden of leadership of the children of Israel in the wilderness; and to bear them upon his heart before the Lord, as high priest. This transformation of so ordinary a man —not dramatically effected, in a moment, but the result of progressive growth in grace through the years—is one of the most inspiring word-pictures coming to us from the Old Testament portrait-gallery.

While only a Moses could be leader of the delivered but unthankful and querulous multitude, it was Aaron whom God appointed as high priest, to minister in His sanctuary as His representative unto the people, and their representative in His presence. His very faults and failings were in a sense a qualification for this office: for his own infirmities made him the more keenly aware of being truly one of the wayward and sinful people, who could have both understanding and compassion as their intercessor with God. For this office, he was clothed with garments "for glory and beauty," typifying the perfections of our Lord Jesus Christ, our great High Priest, whom he foreshadowed.

There came a day when Aaron, who had joined with Miriam in jealous criticism of Moses—yet another instance of his being swayed by a stronger will than his own, which brought a stern rebuke from God—found himself the target of similar jealous criticism on the part of Korah and certain other eminent Levites, who claimed equal privileges with Aaron in the

priesthood. How glad he was of the strong leadership of Moses
in that critical hour! Together they confronted the ambitious
malcontents, having first fallen upon their faces before God: and
the Lord confirmed His choice of Aaron as sole high priest, by
judgment against Korah and his associates, as unmistakably as
He had set His seal upon the supreme office of Moses. This
vindication did not elate Aaron, however; he proved himself to
be a true priest at heart, as well as by the divine appointment:
for when God would have consumed the still-rebellious people,
Aaron ran into the midst of the congregation with a censer, to
make an atonement for the people; and he stood between the
dead and the living, and the plague was stayed (Num. 16).
That was perhaps his finest hour. It is thrilling to officiate at
stately ceremonies, as Aaron did, especially on the great Day
of Atonement; it is heart-stirring to pronounce the blessing of
God upon hushed multitudes of worshipping people; but it is
yet a higher privilege to stand between guilty men and the
merited judgment of God, that grace may accomplish its perfect
work.

After that truly priestly act, came a wondrous token making
his calling and election to his high office doubly sure. In
obedience to the divine command Aaron yielded up his rod,
as the head of the tribe of Levi, to be placed with those of the
heads of the other eleven tribes, before the presence of the Lord,
within the tabernacle. With awed expectancy the entire congregation waited until, the next morning, Aaron's rod was
distinguished from all the others by a miraculous transformation: for it had broken forth into bud and blossom and fruit.
Thus God strengthened his heart, and silenced every opposing
voice.

The sharer with Moses of so many experiences of joy and
sorrow, of testing and triumph, through so many years of
devoted service both to God and the people, Aaron like his
brother forfeited the privilege of entering the Promised Land.
This was the consequence of their sin when together they
disobeyed the divine command and struck the rock instead of
speaking to it. Ruskin describes the final scene of his long life,

in a passage of unmatched beauty and spiritual perception: let us rescue it from the oblivion of its entombment in *Modern Painters*, and introduce it to a generation which knows little of the magic of that master of English prose:

"Try to realise that going forth of Aaron from the midst of the congregation. He who had so often done sacrifice for their sin, going forth now to offer up his own spirit. He who had stood, among them, between the dead and the living, and had seen the eyes of all that great multitude turned to him, that by his intercession their breath might yet be drawn a moment more, going farther now to meet the Angel of Death face to face, and deliver himself into his hand. Try if you cannot walk, in thought, with those two brothers, and the son, as they passed the outmost tents of Israel, and turned while yet the dew lay round about the camp, towards the slopes of Mount Hor; talking together for the last time, as, step by step, they felt the steeper rising of the rocks; and hour after hour, beneath the ascending sun, the horizon grew broader as they climbed, and all the folded hills of Idumea, one by one subdued, showed amidst their hollows in the haze of noon, the windings of that long desert journey, now at last to close. But who shall enter into the thoughts of the High Priest, as his eye followed those paths of ancient pilgrimage; or, through the silence of the arid and endless hills, stretching even to the dim peak of Sinai, the whole history of those forty years was unfolded before him, and the mysteries of his own ministries revealed to him; and that other Holy of Holies, of which the mountain peaks were the altars, and the mountain clouds the veil, the firmament of his Father's dwelling, opened to him still more brightly and infinitely as he drew nearer his death; until at last, on the shadeless summit— from him on whom sin was to be laid no more—from him, on whose heart the names of sinful nations were to press their graven fire no longer—the brother and the son took breastplate and sword, and left him to his rest."

6

Caleb: Whose Zeal Continued Unabated

YOUTH is customarily the time for inspired adventure and reckless bravery; the prime of life, for steady competence. Old age is naturally regarded as the time for the easing of responsibilities and the enjoyment of restful leisure. Some few, however, defy the natural order, and achieve their greatest exploits or rise to the heights of daring and accomplishment in advancing years. Such an one was Caleb. At eighty-five he uttered one of the most heart-stirring speeches in the whole Bible—and followed his noble words with deeds which fully matched them in courage and fiery zeal.

Caleb was always, of course, a man of faith and valour. It is impossible to rise to a great opportunity in old age unless the necessary qualities have been cherished through the preceding years. Crises do not create the requisite traits of character: they test and reveal them. In the case of Caleb these qualities were denied the chance of rising to the heights of their supreme expression until he reached a venerable age. As a man of forty he had shown his sterling character and true godliness, when chosen as the representative of his tribe—Judah—to spy out the land which God had promised the Israelites as their possession. Like his eleven companions, he confirmed that it was indeed a goodly land: but ten of them spoke in terror-struck tones of giants who dwelt there, and affirmed that the children of Israel could never hope to subdue them. Only two had the faith to declare that God, who had wrought such wonders for them thus far, would also give them victory over these inhabitants of the land.

Of these two, Caleb was one. His was an even more notable testimony than that of Joshua; for it was not surprising that the companion and trusted lieutenant of Moses, who had been privileged to share so many outstanding experiences with the great leader of the nation, should be confident that God would fulfil His word and give them the promised land. Moreover, it was Caleb who spoke the words which rang out challengingly to the whole assembled people: "Let us go up at once and possess it; for we are well able to overcome it" (Num. 13: 30). But the people heeded the ten spies who had brought an evil report, and in consequence they were excluded from the land for nearly forty years. And with them, Caleb was kept out of *his* inheritance, through their lack of faith. He was ready to go forward; he was deserving of his inheritance: instead, he had to wait for it for a further forty-five years.

Therein lies a lesson we often tend to overlook: that the spiritual state of the Church as a whole has its effect upon each member thereof. There are numerous stories in Scripture which emphasize the opposite truth: that an individual may exercise an incalculable influence upon the many: but the reverse also is true. We are bound together in the bundle of life, spiritually, as the people of God, as well as in natural and national relationships. While the faith and dedicated service of one might inspire a Church or bring revival to a nation, it is also true that the low ebb of spiritual life generally has its effect upon each believer individually. If the windows of heaven were to be opened and the Church revived, every member of it would share in the blessing. While revival tarries, all have to maintain a life of faith in God despite the prevailing spiritual dearth and the lack of exhilarating experiences.

It is important to recognize this simple fact, for some exponents of holiness teaching suggest that, through the indwelling of the Holy Spirit, each child of God should enjoy the experience of personal "revival" whatever the condition of the Church might be; and that the lack of it is evidence of failure in faith. Believing this, many Christians suffer needless self-reproach. But while complacency with any standard less than "the fullness of the blessing of the Gospel of Christ" (Rom. 15: 29) is to be shunned, yet a recognition of spiritual principles would obviate unnecessary self-condemnation. The inspiring example of Caleb's life is that faith should be cherished un-dimmed and unflagging through all the vicissitudes and testings of the wilderness way. All such will "possess the land" when revival comes.

Caleb saw all his contemporaries save one—Joshua, his sole loyal fellow-spy, and eventually the successor to Moses as the nation's leader—perish in the wilderness. At length the younger generation crossed Jordan and entered the land: yet Caleb still had to wait for his inheritance a further seven years, while the conquest of the Canaanites was proceeding. At last the time arrived for the various tribes to be apportioned their allotted territory, and the hour struck for Caleb's supreme declaration and deeds of faith. He came to Joshua and claimed the possession promised him by God through Moses forty-five years previously. Joshua knew of the promise, and doubtless re-membered it well: but he did not bestow the "blessing" until Caleb claimed it (Joshua 14: 13). The inheritance belonged to Caleb by divine promise; but it was not actually given him until he came forward and petitioned to receive it. That is in accord with all Scriptural teaching. There are given unto the people of God great and precious promises; but these are not fulfilled automatically. Faith is the condition upon which all the promises depend. What is pledged must be claimed if we would possess. We must apprehend that for which we have been apprehended of Christ Jesus (Phil. 3: 12).

The moment of opportunity—which had tarried long—found Caleb with faith undimmed and courage unquenched. He did not say, "I have waited so long that the inheritance is now scarcely worth having. I am old, and all I need is a quiet spot on which to spend a peaceful retirement." Instead, his words are a rebuke to the lethargy of spirit which all too often charac-terizes those nearing the end of life's journey. "Now behold," he said, "the Lord hath kept me alive these forty and five years ... I am as strong this day as I was in the day that Moses sent me ...

Now therefore give me this mountain, whereof the Lord spake in that day" (Joshua 14: 10–12). What thrilling words; what a challenge to faith! He was content with nothing less than the promise of God in all the fullness and grandeur of it. He was prepared to scale the heights and to fight with giants, despite his eighty-five years. Nothing less than God's best for him, in all its length and breadth and height, would suffice the dauntless spirit of Caleb. He had waited long, in steadfast faith: and he had been preserved in strength to possess that which had been preserved by God for him.

Few are able to say that their physical strength remains unaffected by the passing of the years; but spiritually we should all, like Moses the man of God and Caleb his worthy henchman, be able to declare to the end that our vision is as keen as in the days of our youth, and our zeal unabated. For those who are of the spiritual lineage of Caleb prove, like him, that God not only keeps faith alive, but sustains it in strength, unto the fulfilling of all His purposes of grace in Christ.

Claiming the promises is, however, not enough in itself. Faith is to be evidenced not only in words but in deeds. Caleb had not merely to say "give me this mountain," but to ascend it, and drive thence the sons of Anak from their fortified cities. And that he did (Joshua 15: 13, 14). He showed forth his faith by his works. Again he exemplifies an abiding principle. The promises of God do not secure to the Christian an uneventful path way through life; an uncontested possession of his inheritance. There are adversaries to overcome; giants to be dispossessed. But victory is assured, if the battle is entered in true trust in God. Caleb was absolutely confident of victory. He knew that the testimony he had borne so long ago was true: "We are well able to overcome." So he went forward, a man of faith and of war. God had kept him in strength; yet he did not rely upon his own abilities and experience and resources. "If so be the Lord will be with me," he declared, "then I shall be able to drive them out, as the Lord said" (Joshua 14: 12). His confidence in this hour of crucial testing remained steadfastly fixed in God. He knew that He who had promised was faithful, and was able to perform all that He had pledged.

Then, in the conclusion of the story, is a heart-warming enlargement of the scope of the blessing which Caleb received. Having conquered his foes and possessed his inheritance, the veteran warrior uttered a challenge to the younger generation, to follow in his train (Joshua 15: 16). He did not adopt the attitude that, having at last received his due reward, he would settle down and enjoy it selfishly; he remembered still that he was a member of the nation, one of the people of God; and he inspired others also to conquer and to possess.

Finally, his story closes with the request of his daughter Achsah, who married Othniel—later to become the first of the judges: "Give me a blessing," she pleaded—and he gave her "the upper springs, and the nether springs" (Joshua 15: 19). Having been blessed, Caleb was able, out of bounty he had received from the Lord, to bless others. Every blessing of God is given in order to be shared: and in the sharing the full blessedness is experienced. He who seeks to enjoy the goodness of the Lord for himself alone, thereby deprives not only others but also himself, and frustrates the full purposes of God in bestowing the blessing. For God's will is, that having received of His fullness, His people should be communicators of that grace; channels of His blessing. In Caleb was fulfilled the ancient promise of God to Abram, "I will bless thee . . . and thou shalt be a blessing" (Gen. 12: 2).

7

Jonathan: And All History's Most Famous Friendship

B Y every standard we can apply, Jonathan is one of the noblest characters in all Israel's history. In him were found almost all the qualities and virtues most highly esteemed not only by men, but by God Himself. Courageous magnanimous, utterly devoid of guile or jealousy, he also possessed a sincere, soldierly piety. No one was more worthy of a place among the heroes of faith, than this attractive young prince. If we include him among the "lesser lights," it is only in relation to David, with whom his name is immemorially linked.

There is not to be found in all literature, of any race or age, a story of friendship to compare with that of David and Jonathan. Their hearts were knit together in bonds of un-alloyed mutual love and esteem. Such friendship is rare indeed: but practically every human heart yearns to experience it. That is why this story strikes so responsive a chord. In his essay on "Christ's Hospital" Charles Lamb tells of two school-fellows who later became colleagues and life-long companions: and the gentle Elia observes, "Oh, it is pleasant, as it is rare, to find the same arm linked in yours at forty, which at thirteen helped to turn over the *Cicero De Amicitia*, or some tale of Antique Friendship, which the young heart even then was burning to anticipate!" Is there not the wistful note of unrealised desire in that moving sentence? Certainly far greater numbers "burn to anticipate" than actually realise such a friendship. But the very desire is good: the fire of longing is refining.

Jonathan was a little older than David, and had notable exploits to his credit when the shepherd lad came to visit his brothers in Saul's army, and the two future friends met for the first time. The king's son was second in command of the armies of Israel, and had overcome a Philistine garrison—or "pillar," as some Hebrew scholars think the word should be rendered; signifying a standard set up to mark the Philistine supremacy (1 Sam. 13: 2, 3). Later, when Israel was in a state of subjection to the Philistines, his valiant spirit rebelled against such servitude and, with his armour-bearer, he set out upon a venture which, apart from inspired faith in God, would have been suicidal. Saying to his like-minded companion, "Come, and let us go over into the garrison of these uncircumcised: it may be the Lord will work for us: for there is no restraint to the Lord to save by many or by few" (1 Sam. 14: 6), Jonathan scaled a rocky eminence on which was situate an enemy stronghold—in broad daylight, and in full view of the mocking Philistines. It was indeed so amazing a feat that the Philistines assumed they were deserters from the ranks of Israel, and taunted them as such—only to be scattered by the unexpected assault of the two intrepid young heroes. For cool courage, for sublime faith in God, no incident in the Biblical narrative is more illustrious than this: and it was the prelude to a notable victory. Small wonder that the army was devoted to its youthful prince: so much so that, when his life was in jeopardy through the unwitting violation of a rash vow on the part of Saul, they determinedly intervened and exclaimed, "Shall Jonathan die, who hath wrought this great salvation in Israel? God forbid: as the Lord liveth, there shall not one hair of his head fall to the ground: for he hath wrought with God this day." And the historian adds, "So the people rescued Jonathan, that he died not" (14: 45).

Yet this true prince of Israel was shortly afterwards silent and abashed before the taunts of Goliath. And when a youth from the hills of Bethlehem went forth to meet the giant, with five stones and a sling and a trust in God which banished all fear, Jonathan recognized a yet higher degree of faith and courage than his own. He was noble enough to realize the superiority of the lad, and to admire him without jealousy:

and in that moment their friendship was born, for "the soul of Jonathan was knit with the soul of David, and Jonathan loved him as his own soul" (18:1). It is noteworthy that the initiative came from Jonathan—as indeed it must, in the relationship of prince and subject. He showed his regard by stripping off his robe and giving it to David, and his sword, bow, and girdle. It was a mark of signal honour for a royal personage thus to attire a subject—as Pharaoh had robed Joseph in Egypt long years before: but in this case the act of Jonathan probably had a deeper significance. Was it perhaps a tacit acknowledgment that David was more worthy of the royal robes; better qualified to come to the throne, than he?

If that be the case, Jonathan's love for David was the most self-effacing and self-renouncing the world has ever known, save in One whom in many respects Jonathan pre-figures. He knew that his father, Saul, had through disobedience forfeited the throne; for Samuel had plainly told him, "Thou hast done foolishly . . . for now would the Lord have established thy kingdom upon Israel for ever. But now thy kingdom shall not continue: the Lord hath sought Him a man after His own heart. . . . Because thou hast not kept that which the Lord commanded thee" (13: 13, 14). Whether or not Saul learned that the prophet had anointed David as his successor, we do not know: but it soon became apparent that the young vanquisher of Goliath was destined for the throne. Saul's favour toward him turned into a furious, murderous enmity. But if the father had cause for jealousy, Jonathan had more. He had been the beloved young "general" of the army: graceful of person, swift and fearless in action, they named him admiringly "the gazelle" (2 Sam. 1: 19, R.V. marg.); but David now took his place (1 Sam. 18: 7; 19: 8). More than that, Jonathan certainly came to recognise that David would succeed Saul as king; yet never the slightest tinge of jealousy stained his affection for David, or marred his attitude toward him. In a submission to the will of God comparable to that of the great forerunner of the Messiah, he anticipated the declaration, "He must increase, but I must decrease."

A man is known, the old adage avers, by his friends: and there is truth in the saying. The unexampled friendship of these two young men signifies an exceptional kinship of nature. The warm affection, undeviating loyalty, courage to face a lion and a bear, wedded to unwavering faith in God—these qualities which we know so well to have characterised the whole career of David, found their counterpart in Jonathan also. Deep responded unto deep; heart was knit to heart, and soul to soul.

Saul's growing hatred toward David makes Jonathan's constant loyalty to his friend shine the brighter. He pleaded the cause of David with his father, and for a time succeeded in persuading the king to take a reasonable attitude (19: 4–6). But hate once indulged lays hold upon the mind and heart like a canker, and grows insatiably. So it was with Saul, until David realised that the king had determined to kill him. Jonathan, always willing to think the best of another, could not at first believe that his father would go back on the pledge he had given, to make no attack on David (20: 1, 2). And so the two friends devised a means for putting the king's intentions to the test; and when Saul suspected that Jonathan was protecting David, he raised his great war-spear against his own son, in his mad rage, and would have killed him if he could (vv. 30–33). From that time onward David became a fugitive, hounded by Saul with implacable determination to slay him.

This sad episode involved Jonathan in the bitter experience of a heart-rending conflict of loyalties. His father was the open enemy of his dearest friend. He knew that his own prospect of succession to the throne had been destroyed by his father through disobedience to the divine command; and that in persecuting David, Saul was yet further resisting the will of God. Even more, Saul had lifted up his hand in murderous intent against Jonathan himself. Yet Jonathan remained un-swervingly loyal in his filial duty to Saul, even as he remained unwaveringly true to his friendship with David. He did not forsake his father and throw in his lot with the one whom he knew to be God's anointed. Nor did he fail in any respect toward his friend. In a situation which seemed to necessitate a choice between two loyalties, he remained utterly true to both.

In that, he has provided a shining example and inspiration for countless young Christians today who experience a similar struggle of heart. Family ties, deep and strong though they may be, are often opposed to spiritual relationships. Faced with this dilemma, there is a temptation to consider that the two loyalties are incompatible, and that a choice between them must be made; and our Lord's solemn warning that a man's foes shall be those of his own household is sometimes misinterpreted to justify a breach in family relationships. Occasionally a rupture is unavoidable, for antagonism is so strong as to cast out the one who confesses Christ. In every such case the disowned child of God can rest upon the assurance that "when my father and mother forsake me, the Lord will take me up" (Ps. 27: 10). But such a breach should never be precipitated by a professing Christian. Loyalty in earthly relationships should find its fullest expression, unto ultimate lengths of human endurance. Thus Jonathan remained at the side of Saul: never compromising his loyalty to David, never ashamed or afraid to own it, and never doing anything to harm his friend; never assisting Saul in his persecution of David, but, when the king turned his energies against the Philistines, fighting at his side and eventually dying with him. Jonathan was faithful unto death—to God; to Saul, his father and his king; and to his friend. What more glorious epitaph could any man deserve?

One last incident remains, to complete the glowing story of his life and self-denying friendship. During the blackest days of David's hiding from Saul, when his faith was manifestly tested almost to the limit, Jonathan "went to David into the wood, and strengthened his hand in God" (1 Sam. 23: 16). This proved to be their last meeting. It was doubtless made by Jonathan at the risk of his life, for his act would undoubtedly have been regarded by Saul as high treason; and in it he fulfilled the highest privilege of a friend. Here is the supreme expression of friendship: "He strengthened his hand in God." He and David might have fallen upon each other's neck, and enjoyed awhile sweet companionship as an end in itself: instead, Jonathan turned the thoughts of his harassed friend away from themselves, unto God.

How we should like to know just what passed between them! This only we are told: that Jonathan reminded David of the divine promises and the divine faithfulness. "Fear not," he said, "for the hand of Saul my father shall not find thee, and thou shalt be king over Israel . . . and that also my father knoweth" (v. 17). God had promised, and His pledge could not fail of fulfilment. Thus he comforted and reassured the weary fugitive. To "strengthen in God" the hands of a friend is the truest service a man can render another—one which reaches beyond the confines of this life, to the eternal purposes and destiny: and it is possible to all of us, far short as we fall of the stature of a Jonathan! For we all know, at some time or other, a harassed "David" who needs the word which will give new heart of hope and trust—and we can speak it.

Before parting, never to see one another again, "they two made a covenant before the Lord." What a worthy culmination of their true and tender friendship: renewing their vows together in the presence of the Lord. It was because they both were true men of God that they were also such true friends. In this wondrous friendship, Jonathan's had been the dominant part. The initiative of it sprang from him; as a prince, and as an older, more experienced man, he had everything to give and nothing to receive, save the responding love of David. With willing heart he rejoiced in the prospect of his friend being preferred before him. In time of need, he strengthened his hand in God.

Well might David lament the death of such a friend, in immortal elegy. Well might he sing in praise of him, "The beauty of Israel is slain upon thy high places: how are the mighty fallen! O Jonathan . . . I am distressed for thee, my brother Jonathan: very pleasant hast thou been unto me: thy love to me was wonderful, passing the love of women" (2 Sam. 1: 19–27).

David never saw his like again. In the generosity of his heart, he longed to show to others, in his day of power, such friendship as Jonathan had shown to him. But there are few unselfish enough to prove true friends. Indeed, many will take advantage of proffered friendship, and as readily betray it when it suits them. Not without good reason did the prophet of a later day sound out the warning, "trust ye not in a friend . . ." (Mic. 7: 5). David's experience was bitter indeed: "mine own familiar friend," he exclaimed, "in whom I trusted . . . hath lifted up his heel against me" (Ps. 41: 9). And again, "it was not an enemy that reproached me; then I could have borne it: neither was it he that hated me that did magnify himself against me; then I would have hid myself from him. But it was thou, a man mine equal, my guide, my acquaintance. We took sweet counsel together, and walked into the house of God in company . . ." (Ps. 55: 12-14). Yes, it takes two of like mind and heart, whose souls are truly knit, to make a friendship. Very rarely indeed does a David meet a Jonathan.

Must we then yearn for friendship without hope of satisfaction? Has God created within us a capacity almost certain to be denied? Nay! Bible students and expositors throughout the Christian era have seen in Jonathan a foreshadowing of our Lord Jesus Christ, the "Friend who sticketh closer than a brother" (Prov. 18: 24). It is He who takes the initiative in knitting our soul to His; who stoops in grace to call, and make, us His friends. He clothes us with the robes of His righteousness; He lifts us to His very throne. He strengthens our hands in God in every time of adversity and trial. His love is strong and tender, unchangeable, and faithful unto death—even the death of the Cross. He is our Jonathan—if we will be His David

8

Asaph: The Chief Musician

IN the praise of God the human tongue finds its highest employ. Words become weighted with gold when they are addressed in adoration to the Almighty. Spoken words will not suffice, however, to express the devotion of the heart when conscious of the high privilege of worshipping the Maker of heaven and earth. No wonder that David, "the sweet singer of Israel," exclaimed, "Make a joyful noise unto the Lord . . . Come before His presence with singing;" "Sing aloud unto God our strength: make a joyful noise unto the God of Jacob;" "Sing unto Him, sing psalms" . . . for in singing and making melody unto the Lord, His people can more worthily express their devotion, than in sober speech. But even singing will not itself satisfy the desire of truly thankful hearts to exalt and magnify His holy name: the aid of every appropriate musical instrument is summoned to swell the anthem of the redeemed— "Praise the Lord with the harp: sing unto Him with the psaltery and an instrument of ten strings. Sing unto Him a new song; play skilfully with a loud noise."

Doubtless the patriarchs sang on occasion spontaneous outbursts of exalted homage. How could Adam have forborne to sing in Eden, when God drew near in the cool of the day; or Abraham, when he saw the day of Christ and was glad; or Jacob, when the sun rose upon him at Peniel, and he limped forward into the new day a Prince with God? But singing is in Scripture regarded especially as a means of corporate worship by the assembled people of God. It therefore came into its own when Israel, as a nation, realized their privilege as the covenant people.

Moses was the first to lead the newly redeemed nation in singing, after they had crossed the Red Sea; and he composed a psalm for the occasion—thus making the first contribution to the psalmody of Israel, which in course of time became the richest treasury of devotion and worship for all the ransomed of the Lord, of all races and all generations. And from that very beginning of singing the praises of God in unison, music has mingled with the human voice—for "Miriam the prophetess took a timbrel in her hand: and all the women went out after her with timbrels and with dances. And Miriam answered them, Sing ye to the Lord, for He hath triumphed gloriously; the horse and his rider hath He thrown in the sea" (Exod. 15: 1–21). That was the inception of the musical accompaniment of congregational worship from which has developed all the church music of our day.

Musical instruments were not originally devised for purposes of worship. On the contrary, "Jubal (whose name means 'music player') was the father of all such as handle the harp and organ"—and he was of the lineage of Cain, whose ungodly course is recounted in Genesis 4: 16–24. But the gift of music, and of music-making, is from God, and was rightly claimed and consecrated for His service. General William Booth was following a sound principle when he commanded the Salvation Army to make use of well-known tunes in their open-air work, exclaiming, "Why should the devil have all the best tunes!"

We do not know a great deal about the musical aspect of the Tabernacle services, but during the reign of David this manifestly became quite elaborate. Himself a musician as well as a poet, David appointed Asaph as choirmaster and chief of the musicians, to train the choir and orchestra, with a view to their leading the worship of the nation in the temple which David hoped to build. Although he was denied the privilege of erecting that House of God, David prepared for it not only in the gathering and dedicating of treasure and materials, but in cultivating the spirit of worship and formulating the ritual in which it should be expressed. In this, Asaph was his henchman: to

Asaph many of his psalms were addressed, and Asaph himself composed a number of psalms.

A Levite, and therefore from birth dedicated to the service of God, Asaph is first mentioned as one of the three principal musicians (1 Chron. 15: 16–19), and was later promoted to be their chief (16: 5, 7). He also established a "school of sacred music" whose students, "the sons of Asaph"—whether literally his descendants or only metaphorically so, is not certain—became the leaders of the Temple worship for many generations. What a privilege was his, however, in developing the musical aspect of the worship of the elect nation, at that formative period and under the inspired guidance of David! How his heart must have thrilled as he trained the choir and orchestra, and then led them in their praises on that glad day of the bringing of the Ark of the Covenant into Jerusalem! That was his crowning day. Looking back across the centuries we can catch something of the joy and exhilaration of it. Who of us, no matter how unmusical, has not at some time, on hearing a renowned orchestra and massive choir, wished we could stand on the conductor's rostrum and command such glorious melody with our baton! In such an hour the music master reigns supreme. Asaph experienced his "crowded hour of glorious life" in leading the united praises of the rejoicing nation. Nor would we begrudge him his pleasure therein; for there is no happier—nor more privileged—pursuit, than singing the praises of God. "Serve the Lord with gladness," said David, so understandingly; and then set us an example in so doing—"My mouth shall praise Thee with joyful lips."

There is ever a danger, however, that music should become an end in itself; a means of self-gratification rather than the glorifying of God. In many a church music is worshipped, rather than the Lord. David knew better than to allow this: with all his encouragement of the best musical talent, and employment of the fullest range of musical instruments, all was kept strictly subordinate to the supreme purpose, of expressing and aiding the worship of God. Asaph was therefore chosen not only for his musical ability, but primarily because he had a right realization of the place and function of music in the service of the Lord. For Asaph, like David, was a man of God; he is described as a "seer," a man endowed by the Spirit of God for the position and privilege of leading the worship of His people (2 Chron. 29: 30).

Today we tend to depart from this high conception of the place of music in public worship, to one or other of two extremes: either music is regarded as all-important, or it is too casually treated. On the one hand, it deflects worship from God to itself; on the other, it fails to inspire and elevate heart and mind in the adoration of God, as it might. In too many churches, little care and even less prayer is devoted to the choice of the organist: anyone who can play will do! But how vital a part the organist fulfils in our church services; for the organ has nowadays taken the place of the "orchestra" of David's day, and the organist is the modern counterpart of Asaph. The tempo and entire "tone" of a congregation's praise is largely dependent upon the lead given by the organist, whether the instrument be a harmonium in a village chapel, or the costly organ of a stately church or cathedral. The one appointed to fulfil this important part in the worship of the people of God, should be as carefully selected as the preacher; and on his part, should possess a sense of vocation comparable to that of the minister. If it were ever so, we should far less frequently hear complaints of dull services! Men of God are needed at the consoles of organs as well as in the pulpits of all our churches.

In one of her inimitable books of Scottish village life, Isabel Cameron gives a delightful pen-picture of Angus the precentor who, with his tuning fork and ringing tenor voice, led the praise of the small congregation in a highland kirk. He was a shoe-maker, but in "raising the tune" and leading the unaccompanied singing of the metrical psalms—for musical instruments are eschewed in the highland glens—he dominated the assembled group, a man appointed of God to direct the praises of His people. He indeed had a high conception of his office—and so was able to inspire a like spirit of reverent yet rejoicing worship among all present. He was a worthy "son of Asaph."

9

Baruch: Penman of a Prophet

IF some folk of mediocre capacities have attained a measure of greatness through their association with men of genius—as did Aaron—it is also true that many really great men could not have fulfilled their life-work without the devoted aid of self-effacing adherents. In measure, indeed, that is true of all: for no man, no matter how great, is utterly self-sufficient, but realises his full stature and accomplishment only with the aid and support of trustworthy collaborators. Even our Lord chose the Twelve, not only that they might become the "foundation stones" of His Church, but also "that they might be with Him"—and He showed need of them, particularly in Gethsemane. "Ye are they," He had said in the Upper Room, "which have continued with me in my temptations"—words which surely contain not only a deep note of gratitude for their companionship, but also a wistful yearning for the maintenance of it through the ordeal confronting Him. But despite that indication of His true humanity, our Lord was, of course, an exception to the principle of dependence upon others: for it was when the disciples "all forsook Him and fled" that He accomplished His supreme ministry for us men and our salvation. Utterly alone, He took the cup of His Passion from the Father's hand, and proceeded to the Cross, there to bear our sins in His own body on the tree. As representative Man He stood apart from the whole human race, albeit identified with it as its Sin-bearer; and in His sole Person He redeemed the sons of Adam unto God. In the solitary character of His redemptive ministry—as in so many other respects—however, He was unique; for mankind generally the rule holds good, that the association of other minds and hearts and hands is needed for the realization of life's highest accomplishments.

So it was with Jeremiah. And God, who raises up such men to match the hour in which they live, raises up also for them the needed helpmeet. Baruch was as manifestly appointed by God to be the companion of Jeremiah, as that great prophet was called to his exalted office. Together they discharged a joint ministry to the nation and to all subsequent generations; and not to Israel alone, but also to an ever-widening circle of nations and tribes and peoples to whom the Word of the Lord has come. Let us remember, whenever we read Jeremiah, that we have his book only through the faithful penmanship of Baruch. He was to the prophet what Timothy was to Paul of a later day: a son and companion in the faith, beloved and trusted, devoted and dutiful, steadfast and self-effacing.

The few Scriptural references to Baruch are supplemented by more detailed information in the *Antiquities* of Josephus. He was of noble family, his brother becoming chief chamberlain to King Zedekiah, and the king's personal companion in exile (Jer. 51: 59, R.V.); and Josephus adds that Baruch was "highly educated." With such a heritage, it is not surprising that he had lofty ambitions: so much so, indeed, that God had to admonish him through Jeremiah, "Seekest thou great things for thyself? seek them not" (45: 5). That such a man should subdue his personal aspirations, and submit to the humiliations and hazards of association with the unpopular prophet of God, evinces a devotion to the Lord parallel with that of Saul of Tarsus long afterwards, who likewise turned his back upon a career of brilliant promise, at the call of God.

The first mention of Baruch is in connection with Jeremiah's purchase of a field in Anathoth, at a time when the Babylonians were actually besieging Jerusalem—an evidence to the nation that, although the judgment he had foretold was impending, he looked beyond it in faith to the restoration which also he proclaimed. The title deeds of this property he handed to Baruch, to hide in a place of safety for posterity. Jeremiah was in prison, but evidently was allowed to receive visitors: it does not seem that Baruch at this time shared his captivity, but he fearlessly fulfilled the part of a loyal disciple of the man of God (32: 12–14).

This was not the beginning of their friendship, of course; the prophecies in the book of Jeremiah are not in chronological sequence, and in chapter 36 we have the full story of the writing of the oracles which had been given through the prophet over a period of years. Zedekiah's predecessor, Jehoiakim, was as ungodly as he, and as resentful of the prophet's rebukes and warnings: he too thought to silence Jeremiah by shutting him up. It was this incarceration which impelled Jeremiah to commit his message to writing; and for this purpose he called upon the aid of Baruch. It must have cost the young man dear, in pride and hopes of preferment, to throw in his lot with the despised Jeremiah. It meant the death-knell of his ambitions, for the royal house was irreconcilably hostile to the prophet; but Baruch was confronted with an issue as clear as that which, six centuries later, our Lord presented to the rich young ruler— and, unlike that young man, Baruch did not turn away from the divine behest. Sorrowful he may have been, for the renouncing of cherished hopes is never easy; but resolutely he followed the example of Moses and chose to suffer affliction with the people of God, rather than enjoy for a season what this world has to offer. He turned his back upon the prospects presented to a courtier, and became the scribe of a man who had incurred the royal displeasure—but a man whom he was convinced to be an ambassador of the King of kings.

And so, fulfilling the lowly task of an amanuensis, Baruch wrote at Jeremiah's dictation. Then came a sterner test: for the prophet commanded him to go to the temple and read out to the assembled people what he had written. That would focus the attention, and the disfavour, of the king upon himself! Small wonder if Baruch had an inward struggle; but his obedience was the more praiseworthy on that very account. Alone, and fully aware of the consequences which his act would provoke, he went to the temple and read aloud the denunciations of God upon the apostate king and nation, and declared the unwelcome prediction of chastening subjugation and captivity.

The expected sequel ensued: the matter came to the ear of the king, who demanded that the roll be brought and read to him—and one of the most dramatic narratives in the Old Testament tells how the defiant Jehoiakim slashed the roll with his penknife, and threw it into the fire. But the Word of God is not so easily destroyed: hidden by God, Jeremiah and Baruch set to work and rewrote the whole—and added more to it (36: 26, 32)!

The brief prophecy to Baruch (ch. 45) undoubtedly relates to this time, and should be appended to chapter 36. It reflects his inward conflict, in the light of God's own standards and requirements. It was not strange, or sinful, that Baruch should seek great things for himself; nor surprising that he should find his ambition so hard to renounce: but when ambition would conflict with the will of God, it becomes the greatest snare. The realm in which the ambition of Baruch could be realised was corrupt, and under the judgment of God—a judgment swiftly to fall. It was impossible to follow the path along which ambition would lead, and be loyal to God. Baruch was at the cross-roads, and must choose one way or the other. God gave him warning that, if he yielded to the impelling of ambition, he would lose everything in the judgment he was called upon to proclaim; but if instead he renounced all for the Lord's sake, he would gain his life—or rather his soul, as the word should be rendered (45: 5). In Baruch, then, we find exemplified the principle which our Lord Jesus so clearly enunciated when He said, "whosoever will save his life shall lose it: and whosoever will lose his life for my sake, shall find it."

In this incident, as ever, the grace of God shines through the stern demand: for the Lord revealed to the young man enduring this bitter struggle between his earthly hopes and spiritual duty, what this very issue involved for *Himself*. The judgment about to come would break down what God Himself had built; would pluck up what *He* had planted; would be the frustration of *His* ambitions concerning His chosen people (45: 4). In the light of what this situation meant to God, should Baruch be distressed at the wreck of *his* trivial hopes and aspirings? In the place of them, God was giving him the privilege of fellowship with Himself; despised indeed of men, but a servant of God, assured of His "well done."

And Baruch chose that better part. He became, not merely the friend and helper of Jeremiah, but the servant and spokesman of God. What privilege, compared with the puny ambition that cost him so much to forgo! None ever forsook position or prospects, family or friends, for the Lord's sake, but is assured of reward beyond all computation.

From that time onward Baruch was a dedicated man: and what his loyal companionship meant to Jeremiah can easily be imagined. Together they faced the wrath of kings, and shared imprisonments; and when the judgment they foretold fell, they were banished together to Egypt—and the intimacy of the bond between them is indicated by the fact that the recalcitrant leaders of the nation complained that Baruch was unduly influencing the prophet (43: 3). In Egypt, the record ends: tradition avers that after Jeremiah's death there, Baruch went to Babylon; but we have no certain knowledge, and other traditions assert that he died in Egypt. But whatever happened to him, the place he came later to occupy in the esteem of the nation, chastened through captivity, is attested by the fact that the apocryphal book of Baruch was attributed to him. Like so many great servants of God, however, his last days are obscure: the Scriptures are concerned with men's relationship to the purpose and service of God, rather than with personal details of their lives.

Suffice it to say that Baruch is an example of one confronted with the issue which in greater or less degree presents itself to every young Christian: the challenge to unreserved self-surrender to God and His will. Few of us seek "great things," and consequently are apt to think that this message of God to Baruch has little reference to us. But omit those two words, and the challenge becomes more pointed: "Seekest thou . . . *for thyself*? Seek not!" Unlike the rich young ruler, we have no great possessions to renounce; unlike Baruch, we have no expectations of high position and prestige. The attractions of the world make little appeal to us. We need the more grace, then, to understand the inward struggle presented by the call of God to such as these; the more compassionate sympathy in order to strengthen and succour them. But no disciple escapes, in some measure and at some time, the choice between *self* and the will of God. Our desires may be modest—reasonable comfort and legitimate pleasures: but these may stand athwart the full realization of the will of God in our lives.

Now, possessions, ambition, comfort and pleasures are not necessarily hindrances to our spiritual well-being, which we must forsake: on the contrary, they may be God's good gifts to us, to enjoy and to use in His service. God raised Joseph to exalted station in Egypt, and Daniel in Babylon: and there is great need of godly men in high office today. But where these things—or any other—are given first place in life, rather than His will, they become a snare.

The issue is clear: can we truly say to God, in the words of our Lord Jesus—our great example, as well as our Saviour— "Not my will, but Thine be done"? That is never a light matter: it demands the deepest searching of motives, and often the most costly renunciation of cherished desires and hopes. But one over-riding consideration has been clearly enunciated by our Lord: "If any man will come after me, let him deny himself, and take up his cross, and follow me" (Matt. 16: 24).

"Arise and follow me!"
   Who answers to the call?
Not Ruler, Scribe, or Pharisee,
   Proud and regardless all.

"Arise and follow me!"
   The Publican hath heard:
And, by the deep Gennesaret Sea,
   Obeys the Master's word.

Thenceforth in joy and fear,
   Where'er the Saviour trod:
Among the Twelve his place was near
   The Holy One of God.

His is no honour mean,
   For Christ to write and die:
Apostle, Saint, Evangelist,
   His record is on high.

                              HENRY ALFORD.

PART II

SOME OF THE LESSER-KNOWN APOSTLES

Jesus sat down, and the twelve apostles with Him. And He said unto them . . . Ye are they which have continued with me in my temptations—Luke 22: 14, 28.

"Such were the men whom Jesus chose to be with Him while He was on this earth, and to carry on His work after He left it. Such were the men whom the Church celebrates as the "glorious company of the apostles." The praise is merited; but the glory of the twelve was not of this world. In a worldly point of view they were a very insignificant company indeed—a band of poor illiterate Galilean provincials, utterly devoid of social consequence, not likely to be chosen by one having supreme regard to prudential considerations. . . .

"Far from regretting that all were not Peters and Johns, it is rather a matter to be thankful for, that there were diversities of gifts among the first preachers of the Gospel. As a general rule, it is not good when all are leaders. Little men are needed as well as great men; for human nature is onesided, and little men have their peculiar virtues and gifts, and can do some things better than their more celebrated brethren."

A. B. BRUCE.
The Training of the Twelve.

10

Companions of Christ

THE ultimate test of Christianity is the effect which it has upon life and character—does it fulfil its claim to change sons of Adam into sons of God? Since this is so, it is of greatest interest to study the influence of the Lord Jesus upon the lives of those with whom He had contact during His ministry on earth. What He did for them, He can do for any disciple today.

In training the twelve for their task of being the evangelists of His glad tidings, the Lord taught them His deepest lessons by His daily life of fellowship with them. We learn most intimately what Jesus was like from the fact that He changed a son of thunder into the apostle of love; we draw very close to His heart as we read of that one leaning upon His breast in the sacred intimacy of unfeigned devotion and trust.

The lives of Peter, James and John have been very fully revealed to us. If we could suddenly come face to face with them, we should be quite prepared for Peter's blusterous greeting and enthusiastic exaltation of his Master; we should be equally prepared for John's tender solicitude concerning the flock of Christ, and his glowing testimony that the eternal Word, God the Son, bears in the midst of the throne the scars of the wounds by which we are healed. We feel that we know these men as intimately as if we had met them in the flesh. But the other apostles who shared with them the privilege of those days in His company, we do not know so well. Therefore we shall consider the Master in His relationship to these disciples of whom less is recorded, but who came under His re-creating hand. In our view there was not such a discrepancy between

the three—Peter, James, and John—and the remaining apostles,
as some suppose. The three were outstanding men, it is true;
but the others were not mediocre. We must not draw hasty
conclusions from the fact that little is recorded about them
in the Gospels; it was not the purpose of the evangelists to
trace individual histories, but to exalt the Lord Jesus Christ.
Very little is said about Matthew, yet it was he who wrote the
first Gospel; some of his companions are mentioned even less
than he is, but we are persuaded that they nobly fulfilled their
office as apostles, and pioneers of the Gospel. The prominence
given in the records to the three is because their ministry was to
be of an especial nature, and also because they are representative men. People of every type and clime can find points of
contact in these three, and find comfort in the fact that Jesus
made of them not only saints, but fishers of men.

Some writers have asserted that the whole company of the
apostles was made up of men of an inferior calibre. To an
unprejudiced reader of the New Testament this view is unten-
able. Jesus chose His companions with divine skill; the material,
though rough-hewn, was of high intrinsic worth. On the other
hand, but for contact with Him they would have lived and died
as obscure members of a subject nation. Only by His fashioning
was their latent possibility transmuted into grandeur of character, so that they were able to render to their fellow-men a
service the full results of which will be known only in eternity.

The whole company originally had this in common with most
of their countrymen—a keen desire to see the establishment
of Messiah's Kingdom: but, in contrast to the rest, they also
had a willingness to sacrifice all things in order to aid that
purpose. Of course, their conception was sadly wrong, not only
in the early days, but right up to the time of Calvary. We know
how true this was of Judas. Probably the eleven were in complete
agreement with Judas in their motives and conceptions in the
earliest days; but they did not end, as he did, by becoming
traitors. This point is significant, for it illuminates tremendously
both the characters of these men, and also the effect that Jesus
had upon them. During their discipleship the Lord was

constantly, here a little, there a little, stripping away their earth-
bound notions of the Kingdom, and revealing the true nature
of His Person and work. Upon Judas this revelation had the
effect of increasing estrangement from the Master unto his final
act of consummate baseness. Not so with the eleven—although
they clung desperately to their hopes of an immediate earthly
kingdom, even squabbling under the very shadow of the Cross
concerning priority of place therein. But we cannot over-
estimate the influence of the Lord upon them in that they did
not become allies of Judas in his villainy.

Perplexed at the nature of Christ's ministry, the disciples
faced the issues clearly. Events were not developing as they had
hoped; if Jesus were the Messiah, then He was acting in a way
altogether incompatible with their cherished dreams and interpretations of prophecy concerning Him; yet He had claimed
their heart's love, and they could not leave Him, could not be
disloyal, even if they would.

On one occasion He had spoken unusually plainly and
strangely, and all the rest of His followers had forsaken Him;
they alone were left, and He wistfully challenged them, "Will
ye also go away?" They had contemplated that possibility,
and Peter, as their spokesman, gave their decision, "Lord,
to whom shall we go? Thou hast the words of eternal life."
They were disappointed and confused, but they could not leave
Him. They had abandoned all to follow Him, and they had
heard Him speak words which they could not understand, but
which had aroused a response in their deepest being, and a
longing which they could not interpret. It was impossible that
they should become just ordinary folk again; they could not
return to their worldly occupations. They hungered for eternal
life, and they had heard Him speak words which had altered all
things for them, and which alone mattered: it was impossible to
go back to the common task, the trivial round. Those words had
pierced their hearts like arrows of fire, and there they blazed
insatiably—to whom could they go?

The factor which made them into apostles of the Lamb was
His love set upon them. They were sincere in heart, and in spite

of blunderings and ambitions, they truly loved Him, and were anxious to be found in the way of obedience and eternal life. Their sincerity gave Him the opportunity He needed. Their poor and twisted conception of the Messiah and His Kingdom had to give place to the gradual unveiling of the glory of God in the face of Jesus Christ. God was manifest in the flesh, not that He might set up an earthly kingdom in rivalry to Rome, but to deal with the problem of sin, and to establish His heavenly Kingdom in righteousness.

They followed Him part way with halting and reluctant steps as He sought to lead them into this revelation; but it was not until after the Resurrection that they saw and really knew who Jesus is, and what He had come to do. In seeing this, they fell at His feet in worship, and yielded themselves to that ministry of His Spirit in them through which He was able to establish His Church. In the vision of Jesus as Lord we also may walk in the way which the apostles trod before us, and be found living members of that Church which they so faithfully served.

11

Andrew: The First "Fisher of Men"

How great a privilege was that of Andrew and John, in that they were the first disciples of the Lord Jesus Christ! They had been disciples of John the Baptist, and became followers of the Lord when He was pointed out by the forerunner as the One who should come.

The fact that they were disciples of John the Baptist indicates that they were earnest and devout in their expectation of the coming King. The whole of Israel was expecting Messiah's advent: surely now the promised Son of David would come to rescue His throne from the insolent dominance of Rome? But the expectation had become earthly and selfish; the prophecies of His coming had been misinterpreted to suit the worldly ambitions and pride of the leaders of the nation, so that the thoughts and hopes concerning the Messiah were warped and distorted. When He came unto His own, His own people recognized and received Him not. John the Baptist was the Spirit-anointed prophet who came to cry to this expectant yet unprepared generation, grown deaf to the voice of God, "Make straight in the desert a highway for our God." He was the direct antithesis of the haughty religious leaders of his day, and his stern message swept through the land as a purifying breath. It was not attractive to the formally religious mind, for it did not prophesy a golden era of national supremacy for Israel under Messiah's sceptre; it did not foretell in glowing terms the subjugation of the proud Roman conqueror. Nay, it sounded a note which fell harshly upon the ears of Pharisees and Sadducees alike—"Repent." The Messiah, said John, would come fan in hand, to sift the chaff from the wheat; He would baptize in the Spirit and in fire.

This message could not fail to arrest and challenge, as it exposed the falsehoods and shams, the hypocrisy and blindness of the great rival religious sects. The leaders, angered by John's searching words, and unrepentant of their sinfulness, were addressed by him as a "generation of vipers." Such a man does not attract any to be his disciples who are not sterlingly true-hearted and zealous for God and righteousness. Andrew was John's disciple, and must have possessed these qualities.

Of course, not until after Calvary were the earthly ambitions and thoughts of the disciples fully swept away, but Andrew learnt from the Baptist much concerning the coming Messiah. He learnt that the popular conception of Him was wrong; that He was coming to deal with this curse of sin which burdened not only Israel, but the whole race, for John spoke of Him as the One "who taketh away the sin of the world."

Andrew, we may safely affirm, therefore, was more earnest than most of his compatriots; his faith was more pure, and his hope more of a life-directing factor. He waited for the Messiah not vaguely and superstitiously, but actively and in living faith, and was anxious to be found prepared to enter His service at His appearance. He was in no way disloyal to John the Baptist when he forsook him to follow Jesus, for to this end alone had he become his disciple.

Ever memorable was that solemn, dramatic announcement of John, "Behold the Lamb of God!" The first contact with Christ ever stamps its impress deep upon the life and memory; the first blest vision of Him abides alway, growing brighter unto the perfect day. How powerfully this incident affected Andrew's companion, John the beloved, we well know. He ever afterward delighted to think of his Lord as "the Lamb of God," and cherished that Name by which the Saviour had been made known to him.

Andrew must have been similarly stirred in heart, as he and his younger companion followed the retreating figure of Jesus. They followed tremblingly and with throbbing hearts, for if He were indeed the Christ, then they were anxious to know Him and be found in fellowship with Him. All their hopes, all that they were, and had, and hoped to be, all hung upon this moment, this possibility of meeting the Messiah face to face.

Christ knew that they followed, and, turning, He challenged them: "What seek ye?" The Lord Jesus always challenges those who would be His disciples, and His questioning gaze pierces to the very intent of the heart. The answer which the two future apostles gave seems very inadequate to this occasion, for they said, "Master, where dwellest Thou?" But He had read their hearts and knew all that lay behind that simple question, all that which was making their pulses to race and their hearts to burn almost intolerably. They could not commit their surging thoughts to words, but He knew, and responded equally simply and directly, "Come and see."

Andrew had all his life to learn more fully the lessons of this first meeting with Jesus; he had to come into ever-deepening fellowship with the Lord, and see in spirit the meaning of that Name of His, the Lamb of God. He was slow to learn, and passed through devious experiences, but all the days of his discipleship he was understanding more vitally the awe-inspiring truth that God had provided Himself a Lamb. It was not until the bright light of the Cross flooded with illumination the prophetic announcement of John, that he fully knew what it meant that He, Jehovah of Hosts, had become incarnate in the Person of His Son in order that He might bear away the sin of as many as believe on His Name.

Andrew is mentioned but rarely in the Gospel record, but the picture presented of him is very pleasing and consistent. He was not so outstanding a character as his brother Peter, whom he brought to the Lord, but he was always as we have seen him —earnest, unassuming, kindly. His first act after following Him has been an inspiration to personal soul-winners ever since—he led his own brother to the Lord. And although first in point of time, he was willing to take a humbler place among the apostles; there is no hint of jealousy or envy in him. He was content to remain loyally in the background while his more aggressive brother was among the three most intimate companions of Christ, privileged to be with Him on occasions when the others were excluded. To take second place to Peter was a great test of character to Andrew, which reveals him in most attractive light.

It was he who told the Master of the lad who had five barley loaves and two fishes, adding wistfully, "What are they among so many?"; to him Philip came for counsel when he had been approached by the Greeks with the request, "Sir, we would see Jesus." He was one of the small company who asked the Lord for fuller details concerning the destruction of the Temple, and His coming again, of which He had spoken—in every case he is the same humble-minded, approachable, thoughtful, sincere and devoted disciple.

He was one who really responded to that invitation to "Come and see." Seeing dimly at first, he responded to the extent of spiritual perception which had come to him, and was rewarded at last with the vision of glory that excelleth. It was after Calvary that he fully saw; he saw all that men can see of the fullness of that great, incomprehensible title, the Lamb of God.

To us also that invitation comes, ringing through the centuries, but inbreathed anew by the urgent desire of the Ascended Lord in the midst of the Throne. He invites each of us to come to Him, and to see who He is—the Lamb of God, the Living One who became dead, and behold, who is alive for evermore! Shall we not worship Him who died to redeem us, and who ever lives, our Lord and our God.

12

Philip: The Gentle, Sympathetic Disciple

PHILIP was a stolid man. Such as he form the phalanx of the Christian ranks. The disciples of the Lord Jesus include all types of persons—visionaries, ascetics, men of profound thought, fiery men of impetuous action, and hosts beside. But the multitude without number who have borne a good confession have been largely composed of "ordinary" folk. The glorious company of the apostles was wondrously representative of almost every conceivable type; more than one of the twelve might serve as a prototype of that company to which we refer. Philip was one such: a plain man, without brilliance of thought or action.

Philip has the honour of being the first apostle to be *called* by the Lord, two days after John and Andrew had come to Him, and the day following Andrew's missionary service in bringing his brother Peter to the Master. There is something delightful in the story of the call of Philip by Jesus. We read that "Jesus *would go forth*, . . . and findeth Philip." It is one of those illuminating incidents, akin to that which occurred later, when "Jesus *must needs* go through Samaria" in order to meet the needs of the hungry soul of the "woman by the well." The care of Jesus for individuals—for those who might so easily be lightly esteemed and overlooked—is indicated. He found Philip—He looked for him, and called him.

From this we gather that though Philip was one of the few who were awaiting the consolation of Israel, yet there was something in his disposition which kept him from approaching Jesus as Andrew and his companion had done. An earnest inquirer, he was slow in arriving at a decision, and reluctant to take any action on his own initiative. How many are so constituted! The world often despises such people as "mere pawns," but the Lord Jesus does not judge after the manner of men. He sought out Philip, as He seeks out true-hearted men and women today, and invites them in tender word, "Follow me."

Having been found by Jesus, Philip "exercised the divinest prerogative of friendship" (Farrar), and sought out Nathanael, who would probably have remained in seclusion had he not been the subject of an act of personal evangelism. Philip, emulating the Master's loving service, went as His ambassador, and his lips were made the medium of a divine call which meant as much to Nathanael as the personal call of Jesus had meant to Philip.

The earnestness and simplicity of heart and mind which characterized this apostle is demonstrated in the incident concerning the Greeks who came to him saying, "Sir, we would see Jesus." They came to Philip evidently because they considered him to be the most approachable of the disciples—they would not have come without premeditation and much consideration. Their choice was justified; he treated their request with the sympathy of one who was himself an inquirer, who knew the fullness of their hearts and the perplexities of their minds. How exquisitely self-effacing was his action in consulting Andrew, and, together, their appearing in deputation before the Lord! Philip did not, as a small-minded man would have done, officiously "take the matter in hand"; he revealed a fine consciousness of the vital issues involved. He felt that the blessing of the knowledge of Christ could not be refused these seekers; yet they were Greeks, and Jesus was the Messiah of the Hebrews. Philip was puzzled by the position in which the Greeks placed him, and his behaviour commands our high respect.

Like so many of the great company of Christians whom he represents, Philip seemed to linger in the initial stage of the knowledge of Christ Jesus. He rejoiced in His Presence, yet did not enter into the profound depths of the knowledge of God in Christ.

The question which Jesus put to him just prior to the miracle of the feeding of the five thousand, "Whence shall we buy bread, that these may eat?" was an attempt to draw out this loyal, loving disciple into a more vigorous, more daring faith. "This He said to prove him: for He knew what He would do." It was as if He were encouraging Philip to say, "If Thou wilt but speak the word, the need will be met." Instead, the prosaic Philip disappointingly answered, "Two hundred pennyworth of bread is not sufficient."

Yes, disappointingly answered; but he was not rebuked or chided. We will not criticize where the Master did not, for how often we answer and behave disappointingly. How often many people would despise us, and comment cynically and sarcastically upon our stupidities and failures. Yet we can ever come with confidence to the Lord; He knows our frame, He remembers that we are *dust*.

At the Last Supper the Lord had been seeking to make these dull-hearted disciples enter into the fullness of the revelation of His Person and purpose. Though they had been with Him throughout His ministry, which had now drawn to its final hour, their eyes were still holden; a veil was still on their hearts: their conception of Him was still earth-bound.

Judas had departed from their midst to enact the most dastardly deed in the world's history, and Jesus was speaking those wondrous words recorded in John 13: 31 onwards. As He spoke of the Father's home and the way thereto, Thomas bluntly interjected, "Lord, we know not whither Thou goest; and how can we know the way?" Jesus replied, "I am the Way. . . . If ye had known me, ye should have known my Father also."

Philip could not let this pass; it was a challenge to the heart-questioning which had so greatly disturbed him of late, so he expressed the problem which was surging within his mind, and said, "Lord, show us the Father, and it sufficeth us." The Lord answered, "Have I been so long time with you, and yet hast thou not known me, Philip? He that hath seen me hath seen the Father. . . . I am in the Father, and the Father in me."

The disciples had not understood the mystery of the Incarnation. These words of Philip expressed the inward turmoil of the ten, as well as his own. Let us not blame them, for have not we at some time failed to receive in simple faith the revelation contained in His words? Have we not rather expected, in order to dispel our doubts once and for all, a dramatic "Damascus road" experience, a heavenly vision, a celestial revelation— we know not quite what?

We worship God, and believe that Jesus came from God, the promised One who is Himself God. Yet somehow we are so slow to apprehend that in Him dwells the fullness of the Godhead in a bodily Form. God the Father has revealed Himself in His Son, the visible Image of the invisible God. He is the only begotten, the Shekinah: whoso hath seen Him hath seen God, hath seen the Father.

Does the question which Philip asked express the deep longing of your heart: would you see the Father? Then to you the answer avails which was given to this disciple of old. Look to Jesus, and by faith in Him you will discover God in His fullness; and all the needs of your quickened spirit will be met. Let us, as did this disciple after the glorious Resurrection of the Lord, lay all our questionings and inward frets at His feet, and worship with hearts abandoned to Him in love and implicit devotion. Then we shall discover that He is the Way, the Truth, and the Life; the true Way, the living Way, the Way unto the Father.

13

Nathanael: An Israelite without Guile

PERHAPS no higher tribute was ever paid to any man than that of the Lord to Nathanael, "Behold, an Israelite indeed, in whom is no guile." The effect of these words upon Nathanael was striking; they convinced him that Jesus was the Christ. Yet he did not then fully realize that the Lord was God Incarnate, or he would have been even more startled at this commendation.

Our Lord, who never uttered words of flattery, saw to the innermost heart of this Israelite, and pronounced him "guile-less." How disconcerting it would be to many if they were suddenly told that their inmost thoughts were discerned! Yet as a man "thinketh in his heart, so is he." Nathanael's thoughts as he sat under the fig-tree were pure; indeed, there can be little doubt that they were definitely spiritual. Alone, in a hidden corner of a small village, this insignificant member of a subject nation was thinking in terms of eternal verities, and was in fellowship with the living God.

The Lord sees all who have a "secret place"; no one who earnestly sought to be in fellowship with Him has retired to a secluded place, and there remained unobserved by God. He knows the inexpressible yearnings of the heart; and the tender, open, responsive heart has never yet been denied the ministrations of His grace.

It was Philip, himself just called to discipleship, who brought Nathanael to Jesus. The nature of Philip's greeting to Nathanael seems to indicate that they had previously talked together concerning Messiah's coming; probably they had often pondered the prophetic writings, and had wistfully hoped to see the day of His appearing. We can imagine that Nathanael's heart leapt as Philip eagerly said, "We have found Him. . . ." Was the dream that they had so often indulged come true? Yet the wild leap of joy was instantly checked as Philip proceeded, ". . . Jesus of Nazareth."

A cold, haunting chill immediately damped the new-born, exultant hope which had flashed through Nathanael's spirit, and he expressed his fear, "Can any good thing come out of Nazareth?" It is difficult to think, however, that this was just an expression of intolerant prejudice, as is usually suggested, for Nathanael was himself a Galilean; but his conceptions of the Messiah were definite and strong: he expected that He would be of most exalted lineage, and was quite unprepared for such news as was brought by Philip. The question did, however, reflect the opinion of the nation toward Nazareth: it was ever a stumbling-block to the Jews that Jesus came from the despised town in the north. In voicing this prejudice, Nathanael was not more bigoted than most; it is oft-times good to state objections candidly, so long as they are not frivolous, for they can then be better dealt with.

Philip was wise; he knew how deep-seated such prejudices can be, and how they colour the thought and judgments of a man, and that they tend to become deepened and intensified when arguments are mustered against them, no matter how weighty these arguments may be. So he avoided this danger by throwing upon Nathanael the onus of deciding concerning the claims of the Lord Jesus after a personal meeting with Him—he said, "Come and see."

In his ready response to this invitation, Nathanael evinced the guilelessness of character which the Lord so soon afterward commended: he did not sit and expatiate upon the prejudice he had voiced; he came that he might see Him, doubtless trusting that God would reveal to him whether Jesus were the Messiah or not.

An Israelite, indeed! A member of that spiritual "seed" which had entered into covenant relationship with God on the basis of outpoured blood; one who had experienced his Peniel;

one in whom the Jacob-nature had been withered by the divine touch, and who had clung to God, and prevailed. To such an one would the vision of an open heaven be granted, and the way of communion made actual.

The supreme comfort of the Gospel is that it reveals God as tenderly solicitous for each individual personally. He does not deal with men in the mass; He knows His "sheep," and calls them by name. During the three and a half years of His earthly ministry, our Lord was ever singling out those in whose hearts there was a true desire, and a response to His grace—He sought out the woman of Samaria, Zacchæus, and many another.

To Nathanael He said, "Before that Philip called thee, . . . I saw thee"—He had determined that this one should be His disciple before Philip's heart had been filled with missionary zeal. The same concern was manifest in the calling of Philip himself—Jesus sought him out; His love had gone forth also to those whose hearts had responded to the call, "Make straight the way of the Lord." Again, when Andrew brought Peter to Him, Jesus said, "Thou art Simon, . . . thou shalt be called Cephas." The Master's love had preceded the ardour of Andrew, and His work was already begun in the heart of the one who was to become a "Rock."

So today He graciously anticipates the turning of any heart to Him. No one can ever take Him by surprise; whatever petition we may bring, we shall find that He already knows all about us, and all our need, and waits to bless. For even the faith in which we approach Him is not of ourselves; it is the gift of God. Moreover, how great an encouragement this thought is, as we seek to be His witnesses; we do not testify for Him in our own strength, but are co-workers with Him in His fore-ordained purpose of grace.

Nathanael's immediate acknowledgment that Jesus was the Christ seems to some unwarranted by the few words which the Lord addressed to him, in view of the cool reception he had accorded the testimony of Philip. Yet is it strange when we consider who it was that Nathanael met? In the moment of meeting deep answered to deep, and within his spirit the

F

conviction was registered, and he uttered the confession, "Thou art the Son of God; Thou art the King of Israel"—Thou art the promised One, the King of that true Israel, that remnant, of which Thou hast said I am a member.

How wondrous a testimony does this incident bear to the Lord Jesus! Nathanael was a man of pure heart and clear spiritual vision, yet having dogmatic notions as to the Messiah. The facts of the Lord's earthly life were inimical to Nathanael's conceptions, yet this guileless Israelite straightway saw within the personality of Jesus that which shone through the garb of His humanity: unreservedly, in spite of every factor which might militate against it, he confessed that Jesus was the Christ, the Son of God, the divine King.

The answer to the desires of the prophets—the desire of God as it found expression in the hearts of the prophets—was come: God had rent the heavens and come down! The way of fellowship between His throne and our dust had been re-opened in and through the One who had vacated that throne in order to reconcile our dust to Himself, through the Passion of His Cross.

There is a problem of identity concerning Nathanael, for he is not mentioned by that name in the Synoptic Gospels; but he is almost certainly the Bartholomew whose name the Synoptic writers link with that of Philip in their lists of the apostles. It is significant that no mention of Bartholomew is made in John's Gospel; while the reference to Nathanael in chapter 21 implies that he was one of the apostolic band. Most of the apostles had two or more names, in accordance with the common practice of those days; so there is nothing unusual in this case. On these strong grounds, therefore, it is generally agreed that Nathanael and Bartholomew are one and the same man. However, we read nothing more about him, under either name, after the incident in John 1, until the Resurrection had been accomplished; then we find him in the group who joined Peter when he said, "I go a-fishing." We know how that fishing expedition ended, and how afterward the apostles became fishers of men.

Through all the varied experiences of the intervening years, we are persuaded that Nathanael beheld ever more clearly that shining way raised up to the Presence of the Majesty on high. Much was hid from his eyes; he did not know what the consummation would be, but he abode faithful until the full vision of the eternal purpose of God in Christ broke in upon his consciousness. The bright light of the Resurrection revealed everything that had been in shadow before; he saw with unveiled eyes "heaven open, and the angels of God ascending and descending upon the Son of Man."

14

Matthew: The Publican

IT is said that "much is in a name." In modern life this may not often be true, but it is certainly true of Bible names. Of one who is mentioned in the Old Testament it was said, "As his name is, so is he." To several in the New Testament, as also in the Old, new names were given because of some outstanding trait in their character, or to commemorate a triumph of grace in their lives. The new names thus bestowed upon these "twice-named" men are significant and revealing; as their names are, so are they. What transformations are indicated by the fact that Jacob became Israel; Simon became Peter; Joses became Barnabas, and Levi became Matthew.

Levi, of course, was a common name in Israel. When Levi the publican followed Jesus, however, he wanted to mark in a definite manner his severance from his old life and all its associations, so he received the new name, Matthew, which means "Gift of God."

As a publican he had a very unenviable job. True, it was lucrative, but it alienated him from all his countrymen save the outcasts. The taxes which he gathered were paid into the coffers of Rome, and were a galling yoke imposed upon the subject-nation by the proud conquerors. The Jews who entered the employ of the tax-farmers were regarded as traitors, and were ostracized—which resulted in increasing their harshness of mind and manner. In this unenviable rôle, Levi performed his duties at Capernaum: it is possible that our Lord had paid taxes to him, rendering unto Caesar that which was Caesar's.

Whether this was so or not, Levi knew of the Lord Jesus before that memorable day of his call. Publicans were reputed to be pitiless and grasping, but in the heart of Levi a dissatisfaction and a strange desire had been working: the words of the Lord had caused to vibrate within him chords which he had stifled into silence when he had accepted the office of tax-gatherer. He knew that a chance was being offered him to break free from the associations which he inwardly despised, and to realize the noblest aspirations which had ever stirred his breast. If he heeded, the possibilities were so tremendous that he feared to contemplate them; but if he disobeyed, a prospect of sheer blackness and despair awaited him.

The crisis came precipitately—life's big issues usually do: there is a preparation, maybe, but the vital decisions of life have to be determined and acted upon unhesitatingly. One day Jesus said, "Follow me." The command was uncompromising. One trembles to think of what would have happened to Matthew had he disobeyed. To hear His call and to heed not, is to place oneself in danger too awesome to dwell upon.

Matthew celebrated this decision by making a feast, to which he assembled his fellow tax-gatherers—none but "publicans and sinners" would dare to be the guests of one "outside the pale." To these, we may be sure, he bore testimony that even to such an one as himself the possibility of spiritual life and service was offered through the grace of the Lord Jesus Christ.

Henceforth Matthew took his place as one of the twelve, yet never a prominent place. Methinks he felt that he had been disloyal to his nation in serving Rome, and was therefore unworthy to occupy an honoured place in the Kingdom which the Messiah had come to establish.

It is interesting to note that another member of the apostolic band was Simon the Zealot. The Zealots were the extreme nationalist faction who had risen in rebellion against Rome (Acts 5: 37). These men were almost fanatical in their hatred of Rome, and intensely despised their own nationals who entered the employ of the conquerors. Yet in Christ Jesus the ex-Zealot and the erstwhile publican were reconciled. What can be more eloquent in its unveiling of the Person of the Lord Jesus, and His influence upon the hearts and lives of men, than the fact that these two representative men of irreconcilable character and creed became "one in Christ Jesus."

In the Gospel narratives Matthew remains in the background, a quiet, unassuming man. Yet he fulfilled that service which he felt to be within his power, and for which, all unknown to himself, he had been called in the predeterminate counsels of God: he kept a careful record of what Jesus said and did. Accustomed to using the pen, he dedicated his gift of writing to the Master's service; and to him, in the divine providence, we owe the first Gospel.

His history, then, is that of a man who seemed committed to a life of ignominy and reproach, but within whose heart the strivings of the Spirit awakened a desire to break free from the bondage of his past, and recommence life on a loftier plane. The opportunity came, but the decision had to be made instantly; in that crucial moment the issue was decided—and he entered into life more abundant.

In his act of prompt obedience, Matthew experienced that divine grace by which all the past was blotted out; all things had become new. This new life he had received as a gift from God, and he commemorated this great change by assuming his new name. It was a constant reminder of the depths from which he had been saved, and a testimony to the grace which had redeemed him and lifted him to such a height of joy and privilege.

Would you, who read his story, like to change your name—the name by which you know yourself, and by which you are known in heaven? Do you look back upon unrealized dreams and desecrated ideals? Have the habits formed through the years led you into ways which you inwardly despise? Matthew would bring you this message of hope, that there is a gift of God for you, if you will but receive it. It is not too late: the Master is willing to blot out all the past, and make your life afresh. But Matthew would urge you not to delay, but to respond while the Spirit yet strives with you; to rise up and follow Him in whom alone is forgiveness and joyous life.

15

Thomas : The Disciple Who Doubted

THOMAS has been called "the melancholy disciple."
Perhaps we are too apt to "label" people, for the human
make-up is so complex that no one characteristic alone
moulds a man's life and thought. But Thomas was certainly of
a melancholy temperament, and it is helpful to remember this
fact when we consider him. Remember, also, that our knowledge of him is based solely upon happenings which occurred
within a few days of our Lord's Death and Resurrection.

The first recorded incident in which Thomas figured was when
the apostles challenged Christ's determination to go to Bethany
to raise Lazarus. They did not know what He intended to do,
but they remonstrated against His going again to the vicinity
of Jerusalem, because on their last visit the Jews had been
distinctly hostile, and had sought to stone Him. The Lord
replied that until His appointed hour came, no harm could
befall. Thomas saw that his fellow-disciples were hesitating to
accompany the Lord, so he said to them, "Let us also go, that
we may die with Him."

How little Thomas knew of the Passion of Christ, which was
to be accomplished in the days immediately ahead! In the
light of that Passion, his words glow with a meaning which the
speaker did not realize. But they show that, although his failings
were grievous, his love for Christ was deep and true. Jesus had
become All-in-all to him, so that he could not bear to think of
life without Him—it would be barren and meaningless. Yet the
Lord had been speaking with increasing plainness of His
approaching death, and a cloud had seemed to descend upon
Thomas's heart, and render all his being numb. Out of this

cloud of gloom he spoke; the desolate horror of life without Christ had begun to dawn upon his imagination, and chilled his spirit.

Love for Christ is supremely important, but it must be wedded to faith and hope to be effectual unto the saving of the soul. Love is the guiding principle of faith unto the hope of His calling: these three abide eternally. Love alone is not enough; Thomas loved so deeply that he was ready to go to the very death with Christ. But love without faith was ineffectual, for it could not hear what Christ was really saying about His death; it could not perceive that His Cross was to be the gateway to the Throne. Lacking faith, his hope had died, and nothing at all seemed to matter!

As love prompted his first recorded saying, so lack of faith was responsible for the second. It was on the evening of the betrayal, in the upper room; Jesus had spoken of His Father's house, and had added, "Whither I go ye know, and the way ye know." Thomas, perplexed and grieved, said, "Lord, we know not whither Thou goest; and how can we know the way?" He had utterly failed to understand what the Lord had been trying to teach them, yet he was not rebuked, but told, "I am the Way"—the Way to the Father.

Do not hasten to blame Thomas, but ask yourself if you have understood this mystic word of the Lord. He is the Way; in Him and through Him we come to the Father. Do you know the Father? If you know the Son, you also know the Father; in honouring the Son you also honour the Father, of whom He is the visible manifestation.

Jesus had been speaking of His death as the mighty act which would secure for them entrance into the Home of the Father; He was going to prepare a place for them. But He had also told them plainly that He would come again and receive them unto Himself. He asked them, as they believed in God, to believe also in Him.

Thomas failed to respond to any of this discourse as he had failed to respond to our Lord's words concerning His approaching Passion. Through it all he heard only the sound of one dread word—death. It gnawed at his heart, and filled all his thoughts. He loved so greatly that the impending separation sounded the death-knell of all that he held dear. The glorious vista of eternal felicity of which the Lord spoke was unable to break in upon his spiritual sight.

Within a few hours of this quiet fellowship in the upper room, the Lord had been betrayed, arrested, tried, and crucified. Under the strain of those hours in which eternal issues were wrought, Thomas was broken and crushed. Though no coward, his love, unfortified by the power of steadfast endurance which a living faith alone can impart, proved quite unequal to fulfilling his own determination, "Let us go, that we may die with Him." In the Master's hour of need, he, with the other disciples, forsook Him and fled.

Golgotha was not the defeat, but the great consummation of Christ's ministry. He arose! Hallelujah!

The disciples should have been confidently expecting His Resurrection, but they all doubted as lamentably as did the one who has been stigmatized "the doubter." They rejected as "idle tales" the testimony of the women that He had arisen. The majority of them were partially convinced by the clear and ringing testimony of Cleopas and his companion, confirming, as it did, that of the women; but their faith in the Resurrection was made a living reality only when He suddenly appeared in the midst as they were assembled in the upper room, and silenced for ever their qualms and hesitancy with His word, "Peace be unto you."

How came it that Thomas was absent from that gathering? Surely he knew of it, and the hope in which it was convened? Was he obstinately perverse? We cannot say; but his persistence in doubt after hearing the report of the gathering indicates that unbelief had so gripped his heart that he was reluctant to pass out of the cloud of gloom which had enveloped him. However, God has used to His glory Thomas's lack of faith, for the convincing of such an one is a striking confirmation of the actuality of the Resurrection.

Yet I think a deeper note underlies the doubt of Thomas. He

did not say, with a hard and callous heart, "In defiance of every evidence, I refuse to believe"; but his words were uttered out of deep soul-agony and a throbbing, burning, bursting heart, "Would to God I could believe but I *dare not*, unless I see Him, and place my fingers upon His wounds." He had firmly believed that Jesus was the Messiah, and he could not conceive of the Messiah dying; yet he had seen Jesus despised, reviled, pierced—*dead*. Calvary had shattered all that he had believed in and prayed for. The agonized cry was wrung from the depths of his heart, "I dare not believe"—it was too bewildering, too tremendous, too awe-inspiring.

Again, he had seen Jesus raise Lazarus; but a prophet could be used by God to raise others, whereas only God could *rise again* in the power of His own endless life! If Jesus were alive, then He must be God. But there is only one God, and if Jesus is God, then He must be Jehovah. It was not merely that He enjoyed a closer fellowship than most men with God in some special commission and anointing, but was One in Essence, in Being, with the Lord of Hosts.

Moreover, if He were alive as God, then it was with the marks and authority of death—Thomas saw something of what Calvary implied. Henceforth the outstanding attribute of God would not be His omnipotent sovereignty, but His Passion—the print of the nails, and all that they imply. Thomas was not more superficial than his brother apostles, but perhaps he saw more of the full import of Calvary; it was he who gave the first full ascription of Deity to Christ when he saw Him, and fell at His feet in glad homage, his fetters for ever cast away, and said, "My Lord and my God."

The Master tenderly received and gently rebuked His erring servant, saying, "Blessed are they that have not seen, and yet have believed."

We have fallen into the habit of using the expression, "doubting Thomas," concerning those who refuse to accept the many infallible proofs of our Lord's Resurrection. But a comparison between them and Thomas cannot be made, for conditions are very different.

The real difficulties which hindered Thomas from believing do not now exist, since the fact of the Resurrection is one of the best-attested events in history. Although we have not seen Him in the flesh, we have seen the operation of His Spirit in works of mercy and redeeming grace. We are not called upon to believe blindly, but to accept what is most clearly proven and rational. Thomas *did* believe when he saw the Lord, but those who refuse his testimony to-day do so in defiance of evidence no less real than that which convinced Thomas, and stand condemned by the apostle under whose hesitancy they think to shelter. To reject the Lord Jesus is to spurn His outstretched, pierced hand.

Shall we not be urgent to assure ourselves that we are found among the company of those who, having not seen, yet believe?

16

Judas: Who Betrayed His Lord

J UDAS. What a picture is conjured up by the name! Through the consummate baseness of one man, the very name has been rendered anathema. Our world's history has been stained with an almost unbroken succession of foul deeds, but the one which stands out starkly from all others in the horror of its hellish foulness, is the betrayal of the Son of Man with a kiss.

Why, then, should the story of the traitor be included with those of the noble men and women who through faith "wrought righteousness"? Well, Judas was numbered by the Lord among His chosen apostles; and the awesome warning of his career presents a salutary challenge amid the inspiring records of those who "obtained a good report" (Heb. 11: 2).

I do not now propose to dwell upon the oft-considered details of his final act of treachery, but to think of the three and a half years which preceded it, and the influence of Judas upon his eleven companions in the apostolic office, and of the Lord Jesus Christ upon Judas.

The question has often been asked, Why did Judas become a disciple of Jesus? Unquestionably he was persuaded that Jesus was the Messiah, and thought that He would speedily establish on earth His victorious Kingdom. Judas was an opportunist, and thought that close association with Him in the days prior to His public recognition as King would ensure for himself an elevated position in the coming régime.

The further question follows, Why did the Lord accept such an one to be His disciple? Well, the other disciples had very similar ideas not only when they first left all to follow Him, but right on to the very eve of the crucifixion. Yet the Lord chose them, and they eventually proved worthy, although so blind throughout those years of His public ministry. The difference between the eleven and Judas was that their earthly ambitions were subservient to a love and zeal for God, a true spirituality and fervent desire to see Him glorified and His purposes realized: but Judas was wholly blind to every consideration except his own gain; the coming Kingdom meant nothing to him apart from an opportunity for self-advancement.

During the first year of His ministry, the popularity of Jesus seemed to indicate that their expectations were well-founded; but the second year was a period of testing and gradual revealing of the true nature of Christ's Kingdom. By the end of that year Judas had revealed himself, and our Lord was constrained to say, "Have not I chosen you twelve, and one of you is a devil?" This stern word was an attempt to sting Judas into a full consciousness of the awful sin which was possessing his heart, that he might recoil from it; but Judas was unrelenting.

During these two years the eleven had become utterly devoted to the Lord, whom they now knew so intimately; they loved Him for His own sake, as well as for the blessings He bestowed. Into their dull hearts had shined some glimmerings of the glory which excelleth, the light divine: His words had awakened a response within their spirits, and they knew that they were "spirit and life."

But while the eleven were thus growing increasingly devoted to Jesus, in spite of evidences that their earthly ambitions were not likely to be realized, the heart of Judas was becoming increasingly bitter and callous. His selfish ambition was so strong that the prospect of it coming to naught caused a sense of frustration to chafe within him, and to break forth in rage against the One in whom he had placed vain hopes. He remained among His followers, perhaps in the hope that Jesus would yet proclaim Himself King, but his heart was growing blacker and more sinister.

The influence of a strong-willed malcontent among a group of men is well known, and as the canker was eating into the heart of Judas, he must have disseminated much poison among his fellow-apostles. The scene at Bethany, when Mary broke her alabastron of ointment at the feet of Jesus, in token of her love and worship, bears witness to this: Judas was the one who inspired the malicious protest against such "waste"—and his motive in so doing was one of theft.

Again, the fact that Jesus chose three—Peter, James, and John—to be His most intimate companions was a test to the rest of the apostles. They could not but notice it, and it is hardly likely that Judas failed to insinuate that it was unfair, and a personal slight to them. Probably this choice of the three was one of the factors which aroused the ire of Judas; he was utterly selfish, and egotistical people always think that they should have first place, and are quick to imagine themselves wronged. This desire for premier place underlay all his actions.

To his eight companions, his arguments would sound very convincing; yet as his spirit grew increasingly black and bitter, they retained the integrity of their loyalty to the Master. In this we discern the Lord's character very luminously; if He could retain their loyalty and love in spite of undeniable ground for the working of evil suggestion, and in spite of the constant evil companionship of the "devil" Judas, then He must have been such an One as possessed the attributes of God, even though He was found in fashion as a Man.

The Lord "knew who should betray Him." It baffles the imagination to conceive what the constant presence of this man must have meant to Him as he watched the growing hostility of Judas: we are amazed at His longsuffering and His loving endeavour to save this abandoned soul from the path which he had chosen. But even although the choice was irrevocably made and the destiny fixed by Judas's own deliberate decision, the Lord did not cast him off, but rather exerted all the appeal of His love—divine love, which does not relax its endeavour to save until the twelfth hour strikes—toward this wretched, gain-cankered soul.

In giving the sop at the Last Supper, the token of affection and esteem—the gesture of the host to the honoured guest—our Lord was not merely giving the sign they had asked (for the rest did not know why Judas went out immediately afterward), but was making the last supreme effort to melt this stony heart. If love could have won Judas, this act would have quickened him to remorse; but unmoved, and set in his evil purpose, Judas was at length told wistfully, searchingly, sadly, "That thou doest, do quickly." So he went out; and it was night—a night that, for him, had no dawn.

We shudder at this story, and well we might. Let us learn therefrom two lessons: first that if we indulge thoughts of self-seeking in our heart, in that lies the seed of the sin of Judas. We are each, apart from His grace, a potential Judas. It is awfully possible to confess Him, and be known for years as His disciple, and in the end to be His enemy. Our only safety lies in an utter abandonment to Him; a laying down of self-desire and ambition, and in place of this, to love Him fervently with unfeigned devotion.

The second lesson is of great comfort: from the fact that our Lord preserved the eleven from "a sin unto death," we learn that He can keep us through every test and every device of the devil, if only we truly love Him. Love Him, give yourself wholly to Him, and you will find in Him your delight and safety—He will save you from all danger, and unto fellowship with Himself which will grow more real and vital unto the breaking of the day when we shall see Him face to face, all shadows for ever fled away.

O God, the Rock of Ages,
  Who evermore hast been
What time the tempest rages,
  Our dwelling-place serene;
Before Thy first creations,
  O Lord, the same as now;
To endless generations
  The everlasting Thou!

Our years are like the shadows
  On sunny hills that lie,
Or grasses in the meadow
  That blossom but to die;
A sleep, a dream, a story
  By strangers quickly told,
An unremaining glory
  Of things that soon are old.

O Thou who canst not slumber,
  Whose light grows never pale,
Teach us aright to number
  Our years before they fail,
On us Thy mercy lighten
  On us Thy goodness rest,
And let Thy Spirit brighten
  The hearts Thyself hast blessed.

Lord, crown our faith's endeavour
  With beauty and with grace,
Till, clothed in light forever,
  We see Thee face to face;
A joy no language measures,
  A fountain brimming o'er
And endless flow of pleasures,
  An ocean without shore.

EDWARD HENRY BICKERSTETH.

PART III

SOME NEW TESTAMENT SAINTS

Them that are sanctified in Christ Jesus, called to be saints—
1 Corinthians 1: 2.

"We seem, by an effort of imagination, to see, as through a bright cloud, the faces of the company (to whom Paul was writing), and to catch the far-off voices; but the dream 'dissolves in wrecks'; we do not know them, we do not know their distant world. But we do know Him in whom they were, and are; and that they have been 'with Him, which is far better,' for now so long a time of rest and glory. Some no doubt by deaths of terror and wonder, by the fire, by the horrible wild beasts, 'departed to be with Him'; some went, perhaps, with a dismissal as gentle as love and stillness could make it. But however, they were the Lord's; they are with the Lord. And we, in Him,

> Are tending upward too,
> As fast as time can move.

So we watch this unknown yet well-beloved company, with a sense of fellowship and expectation impossible out of Christ."

H. C. G. MOULE.
Romans.

17

Simeon and Anna: Witnesses Unto the Christ

THE Christmas stories have a charm unequalled in all
literature. They possess all the delight of the fairy-story,
with this great difference, that these are *true*. Stories of
other-worldly visitants to earth abound in the ancient myth-
ologies: but these highest flights of man's imagination cannot
compare even in beauty of language and ethereal grace, with the
simple record of the events accompanying our Saviour's birth.
None is so thrillingly empyreal and so wondrously tender as
the unadorned narratives of Gabriel's visits to an aged priest as he
ministered at the golden altar of incense; to a Galilean maiden;
and later to her betrothed, the village carpenter who was nevertheless the heir of the house of David. Nor can the finest fiction
of any race or age stir the heart to its profoundest depths like
the artless account of the young couple's journey to Bethlehem
in compliance with the decree of Caesar Augustus; of the babe
born in a stable and cradled in a manger; of the angelic host
announcing the wondrous birth to astounded shepherds; of the
wise men from afar, and their costly gifts; and finally, of the
adoration of the babe in the Temple, by Simeon and Anna.

In fulfilment of the Mosaic requirement that every firstborn
son should be "presented unto the Lord," Jesus was brought by
Joseph and Mary to the Temple, when about six weeks old. It
was a ceremony of a twofold character: of purification and
dedication. A woman was ceremonially unclean for forty days
after the birth of a child. This "impurity" was a consequence
and reminder of the state of sin in which every member of the
fallen human race is born. The child was involved in this
impurity, and so an offering had to be presented—a lamb by

those who could afford it, or a pigeon by poorer people, such as Mary and Joseph—for *their* purification, i.e., of both mother and child (Luke 2: 22, R.V.). In His self-identification with the sinful race of man—albeit through Virgin Birth by the Holy Ghost untainted with spot of sin—the Son of God took upon Himself our impurity, in order that He might purge us from it in His redeeming work. In token of that purifying purpose He was presented unto God as a babe. But more than that: every firstborn son in Israel was thus presented unto the Lord, in acknowledgment of His claim upon the life, instituted when He spared the firstborn who sheltered under the blood of the Passover lamb, on that dread night when all else in Egypt perished. Henceforward God required the firstborn sons of the ransomed race, for His service. In place of those of other tribes, however, the entire tribe of Levi was substituted; and those thereby exempt were ceremonially "presented unto the Lord" in recognition of His claim, and then "redeemed" through sacrifice. So with the infant Jesus: but in His case the presentation was truly unto a life of dedication to the will and service of God.

Thus it was that "the Saviour promised long" came to His Temple; and He was there greeted and acclaimed by two lowly and devout Israelites, representatives of those who "looked for redemption in Jerusalem." It is significant indeed—and a foreshadowing of future events—that the Temple authorities failed to recognize who it was presented unto the Lord that day; they saw no difference in Him from the other infant boys thus brought from all parts of the land by their parents. The priest on duty presumably fulfilled his appointed task; and concerning the ceremony the Evangelist has only this to say—"When they (Joseph and Mary) had performed all things according to the Law of the Lord. . . ." As Isaiah had foretold, the leaders of the nation saw no beauty in Him—no manifest splendour; nothing to mark Him out as the long-awaited Messiah. But God has His own ways of fulfilling His purposes and making known His grace, and often by-passes the official ministry of the Church when it is decadent and spiritually dead—as, alas, it too often has been, and is—and uses those whom His Spirit appoints and anoints, albeit lacking official status. For this high privilege on this occasion, Simeon was chosen. Although not a priest, so far as we know, he fulfilled a true priest's part, in taking the babe in his arms, and blessing Him.

Not only was he God's true priest for this special occasion, but His prophet also. It is often said, concerning the ministry of John the Baptist, that his was the first prophetic voice in Israel for four hundred years. That may be true, in the sense of public ministry recognized throughout the nation as resuscitating the authentic prophetic line. Yet surely the songs associated with the birth of Jesus were prophetic utterances, equally inspired by the Spirit of God as were the oracles through Old Testament seers? Elizabeth's exclamation of glad welcome to her young cousin, "the mother of my Lord"; Mary's *Magnificat*; the *Benedictus* of the loosened tongue of Zacharias; the *Nunc Dimittis* of Simeon—these all attested that "God has visited and redeemed His people."

Who this Simeon was, we do not know. There has been much speculation, including the supposition that he was the father of Gamaliel, who afterwards appears in the Gospel story (Acts 5: 34; 22: 3). This is most improbable, however, and all such guesses are valueless. We are told only that he was "just and devout, waiting for the consolation of Israel; and the Holy Ghost was upon him." Just and devout—righteous in character and conduct; diligent and reverent in religious observances. Many people have one or other of these characteristics: how blessed it is when both are found together! Upright and godly— the twofold aspect of the truly holy life. Rightly adjusted to God and to men. What a wealth of example and implicit exhortation lie in those two simple words!

There were few such men in Israel. Spiritual life was at lowest ebb. Religious observances were never more punctilious, and petty rules and regulations affecting every phase and aspect of life were a yoke grievous to be borne: but true love and fear of God were almost extinguished thereby. Yet God, who even in Elijah's day had seven thousand who refused to bow the knee

to Baal, had still the "remnant" of His elect: and among those
"waiting for the consolation of Israel" was Simeon. He cherished
the promises of the coming Messiah—not, as most of his fellow-
countrymen did, in terms of national aggrandisement at the
expense of other nations, but as the One who would bring
comfort through "speaking to the heart" concerning its
deepest needs (Isa. 40: 1, 2, marg.). There is indeed a twofold
ministry indicated in the word "consolation"—not only comfort, but also counsel (Isa. 9: 6). The babe in Simeon's arms
was the wisdom of God—the Wonderful Counsellor—as well as
the Saviour of the world.

No soul ever seeks God in vain, or endeavours to serve Him
unaided. Simeon, just and devout in an ungodly though
deeply religious generation, possessed what priests and learned
doctors of the law lacked; for the "Holy Ghost was upon him."
And the Spirit of God revealed to him a secret: "that he should
not see death before he had seen the Lord's Christ." We are
not explicitly told that he was elderly, though that is an in-
ference of the remarks concerning him; but he had this promise,
that in his lifetime the Messiah would come, and he would be
privileged to behold him. Now many were looking for the
Christ: but their conceptions were warped by ambitions of
worldly glory, so that when repeated signs pointed to the lowly
babe in Bethlehem, they despised and rejected them—and Him.
But Simeon, taught of God, recognized in that babe the fulfilment of Isaiah's wondrous prophecies. Taking Him in his
arms, he uttered the cry of satisfied expectation, "Lord, now
lettest Thou Thy servant depart in peace, according to Thy
Word." (Incidentally nothing perplexes Free Churchmen more
than the lusty singing of these words weekly by young folk
possessing every zest for life!)

Simeon spoke of himself as a servant appointed to keep watch
through the long hours of darkness, until the dawn should come;
now at length he greeted the Daybreak, his vigil ended. "For
mine eyes have seen Thy salvation." He saw, prophetically
as it were, the realization of the purposes of God in His Sent
One. With the daring of faith he proclaimed God's work

accomplished: for the salvation of His people is secured and guaranteed in and by His Anointed. Moreover, he discerned the wide sweep and comprehensive range of the redeeming grace of God; here was no bigoted Israelite, but a true son of Abraham, to whom God had said, "in thee shall all families of the earth be blessed." Israel as a people had lost that vision, and indeed had no desire to be a channel of blessing to the world: on the contrary, they wished to exclude all the despised Gentiles from the divine blessings—which they claimed, instead, exclusively for themselves. Thereby they forfeited their own blessedness, and were cut off by the God in whom they boasted, while His purposes were fulfilled in and through the Gentiles whom they scorned.

Simeon realized something at least of this, for he acclaimed Jesus, not as a triumphant King of Israel, but "Thy salvation, which Thou hast prepared before the face of all people. . . ." and went on to *place the Gentiles first*—"A light to lighten the Gentiles, and the glory of Thy people Israel." Yes, Israel has its place in the purposes of God, for He has not cast off His elect: Israel shall yet confess in Jesus their Messiah and their glory.

No wonder that Joseph and Mary, despite all they knew and had experienced, should marvel at this prophetic utterance, this priestly benediction, of the devout Simeon! Becoming aware of their wonderment, Simeon addressed them in words still more surprising. First he blessed them—again fulfilling a priestly ministry—and said to Mary, "Behold, this child is set for the fall and rising again of many in Israel; and for a sign which shall be spoken against." Strange words indeed, concerning One whom he had just declared to be "Thy salvation"! How far was this from the popular conception of the hero-king who would expel the Romans and exalt Israel to supremacy among the nations! How different, indeed, from the thoughts and aspirations of Joseph and Mary themselves!

It is one of the principles of Biblical prophecy, however, that many of the predictions of future events could not be fully understood until those events actually come to pass. In the fulfilment, the discerning students of the Scriptures would recognize and understand the unfolding purposes of God. At this early stage of our Lord's earthly life, none could really apprehend the character of Messiah's ministry. Simeon himself, like the prophets before him, spoke by inspiration of the Spirit without foreseeing precisely how his words would come to pass. But he realized at least that in this babe the seemingly contradictory prophecies of Isaiah and others of the prophets would be fulfilled. He would be both the Saviour and the Sovereign; the Redeemer and the Rejected; the Suffering Servant yet the triumphant Lord. He would be the deciding factor in every life; the arbiter of eternal destiny; the stone of stumbling to those who rejected Him, but the foundation stone of saving faith to all who believed.

Finally, in a word tender in fact as it was seemingly harsh, Simeon forewarned Mary that the rosy dreams she cherished would give place to bitter questionings and inexpressible sorrow —"Yea, a sword shall pierce through thy own soul also." Poor Mary, most favoured among women, indeed came to know the most poignant sorrow—until the glad day arrived at length when she recognized in her son her Saviour, and worshipped Him as her God.

Under the law, two witnesses were required to make valid attestation of any fact or event. In observance of that law which He had Himself instituted, God provided two witnesses to His Son, on this occasion of His official presentation in the Temple. Two lowly Israelites, yet knowing the secret of the Lord; a man and a woman—representative of the humble people of God, of both sexes, through all generations.

Anna was "the daughter of Phanuel, of the tribe of Aser," i.e., Ashur, one of the "lost" ten tribes, a few members of which remained in Judah, cherishing their genealogies back through the centuries. All Israel was thus represented on this occasion. Anna was very aged—whether eighty-four years old, as many think, or a widow for eighty-four years, which would make her well over a hundred, is inconclusive; but she spent practically all her time in the Temple, "serving God with fasting and prayers night and day." She is also described as "a prophetess."

Coming in, as Simeon had done, by the leading of the Spirit, she likewise "gave thanks unto the Lord," and "spake of Him unto all that looked for redemption in Jerusalem."

Temple officials might have observed these happenings wondering, and perhaps scorning, and possibly resentful of any intrusion into their privileged domain—but more probably completely unheeding of what they regarded as mere effusions over a winsome babe. Priests who should have recognized the Lord of Glory, merely mumbled their appointed office over yet another infant presented by happy parents for the customary ceremonies. But in the mouth of two witnesses the Christ had been officially acclaimed at His presentation before God and dedication unto His great mission—which should reach out unto all peoples and all generations, a light to lighten the Gentiles and the glory of His people Israel.

18

Philip : The Evangelist

NOT infrequently great privilege in the Kingdom falls to
the lot of seemingly insignificant people. Stephen and
Philip were among the seven men chosen to relieve the
apostles of the more mundane responsibilities in the early
Church; to look after certain "practical" affairs. But they were
marked out for highest spiritual service. Stephen preached with
such power and conviction that he drew upon himself the hatred
of the Jewish authorities almost equal in venom to that they had
manifested toward the Lord Himself; and he followed his Master
in faithfulness unto death, becoming the first Christian martyr.
Philip, too, graduated from deacon to preacher, and was so
effective a missionary that he became known as "*the* evangelist"
(Acts 21 : 8). The early Church chose well, in selecting its first
"diaconate." Business ability and administrative skill were not
regarded as the most desirable qualifications, but rather they
sought men "full of faith and of the Holy Ghost" (Acts 6: 5).
Would that this example had been more closely followed
throughout the history of the Church!

Probably both Stephen and Philip were Hellenist Jews—
Jews born and bred outside Palestine, and where Greek culture
prevailed, as their Greek names indicate; consequently they
were less rigid in their views than their fellow-believers who had
been reared in the strictest traditions and prejudices of Judaism.
This more liberal early influence prepared Philip for the great
service he was to render as the first herald of the glad tidings
among the Samaritans and the Gentiles. Indeed, he was the
very first to fulfil the Lord's command to preach the Gospel
". . . in Samaria, and unto the uttermost parts of the earth,"

i.e. to Gentiles. In this he was the forerunner of both Peter, whose privilege it was to "open the door of faith to the Gentiles" (Acts 14: 27) and of Paul, the apostle of the Gentiles (Rom. 11: 13).

It was the outbreak of persecution against the Church in Jerusalem which ensued upon the martyrdom of Stephen, that led to the "scattering abroad" of its members, and initiated the missionary movement; for they "went everywhere preaching the Word" (Acts 8: 4). Thus began the dispersion of the Church, which proved a most potent factor in its enlargement. It is noteworthy that, whereas the dispersion of the Jews among the Gentiles, intended by God for the blessing of the nations, resulted only in emphasizing the exclusiveness of the Jews—their synagogues became everywhere symbols of their supercilious sense of spiritual superiority, rather than centres of witness to the true God—the dispersion of the Church became a movement of extensive evangelism.

Any other than Spirit-filled men and women might well have been intimidated by the events which, instead, spurred these early Christians to wider evangelistic activity. Philip was undaunted by the death of his friend and colleague; unheeding of the like fate which might overtake him: he preached the same message as Stephen had proclaimed, and with similar forcefulness and courage. But the result in his case was very different, for he went to the Samaritans, less bigoted than the Jews—and they "with one accord gave heed" (v. 6).

Now it was no easy matter for a Jew, albeit an Hellenist, to preach to the Samaritans: for the enmity between the two peoples was intense, as the Gospels affirm and illustrate. The Jews, despising all Gentiles, had an especial scorn for Samaritans, whom they regarded as "half-breeds"—and in every age that has been a term of peculiar ignominy. So extreme was this loathing that the Jews denied the Samaritans the right which they grudgingly permitted to Gentiles, of becoming proselytes to the Jewish faith. In going to the Samaritans and preaching Christ, therefore, Philip was showing forth the spirit of his Lord, as well as following in His steps.

Philip found Samaria in the thrall of a sorcerer named Simon; but the miracles which attended the preaching of the evangelist convinced not only the people but even Simon himself of the truth of the Gospel, so that many were baptised. This is not the occasion to discuss the illuminating story of Simon, and his desire to obtain the power of the Holy Ghost for his own advantage: but his recognition of true spiritual power manifest in the words and deeds of Philip, in contrast to his own spurious arts, is itself a most convincing testimony to Philip's ministry. However, pioneer as he was in gaining the first non-Jewish converts to the Christian faith, it was reserved to Peter to initiate them into membership of the Church, in fulfilment of the Lord's explicit commission (Matt. 16: 19).

Hearing of the events in Samaria, the apostles in Jerusalem sent Peter and John, who "laid their hands on them, and they received the Holy Ghost" (Acts 8: 17). Again, any other than a Spirit-filled man might well have felt a tinge of jealousy that others should come and consummate his work: but there is no hint of it in the record, on the part of Philip. He rejoiced to be used of God, however He might appoint, and in fellowship with whomsoever He might choose. This is demonstrated by his accompanying the apostles on their return to Jerusalem, and sharing with them the joyous task of preaching in many villages of the Samaritans as they went—for that is the implication of verse 25, according to Professor F. F. Bruce, in his scholarly commentary on the Acts. However that may be, the fact that Philip was forthwith used by God to the conversion of the Ethiopian eunuch is sufficient to prove that he had not grieved the Holy Spirit by any unworthy attitude of mind or heart, as in that case he would have become unfitted for such a task. Indeed, the very suggestion that he might have felt some resentment is completely foreign to the tenor of the narrative; the entire "atmosphere" of the story is that of men of God rejoicing together in the work of God. Their attitude exemplifies the principle enunciated later by Paul, that one might sow and another water, but it is *God* who gives the increase. It was their privilege to be labourers together with God. When we think

of the divisions among Christians, and distractions to the
witness of the Church caused through personal jealousies, well
might we pray that this spirit should animate all Christian work
and workers!

From a "mass movement" in Samaria Philip was summoned
by God Himself, through an angel, to a specific task of personal
evangelism: and in the sight of God the winning of one traveller
in the desert was manifestly as important as preaching to the
many in the city. And here again the magnanimous spirit of
Philip shines forth. The qualities which had fitted him so
remarkably for the work in Samaria, led to his selection by
God for this momentous meeting with the Ethiopian eunuch.
This Gentile was a proselyte to the Jewish faith, and had been
up to Jerusalem to worship; so he was in a rather different
category from "Gentiles" as such. Yet he would be treated with
reserve and disdain by the Jewish authorities, despite the fact
that he held an important office at the court of Queen Candace:
for he was a descendant of Ham, a despised race (Num. 12: 1),
and as a eunuch he was disbarred from the full status even of a
proselyte (Deut. 23: 1); he would be a "proselyte of the
gate" with very limited privileges. Such was his hunger for
God, however, that this influential man was ready to submit
to snubs and humiliation at the hands of the Jews, since he was
persuaded that Jehovah their God was the one true and living
God, and that in their Scriptures He had given them His word.

Not one of the apostles, we may infer, was as yet sufficiently
free from the prejudices of their race to be able to lead this wistful, questing soul into the knowledge of Christ not only as the
Messiah of the Jews but the Saviour of the world. Some time
afterwards, it took the vision of the sheet let down from heaven,
to prepare Peter for his visit to Cornelius: and all Peter's elo-
quence to convince his fellow-apostles that he had acted rightly
in going! What a tribute it is to the character of Philip, then,
that he was chosen for this crucial encounter with a Gentile. And
how admirably he fulfilled his task! Within a short chariot
drive in the desert, the man was led to faith in Christ, was
baptised, and proceeded on his way rejoicing.

Philip did not return to Samaria—we do not know why—but went to Caesarea, preaching in all the cities through which he passed (v. 40). Then, after these two stirring episodes, we read nothing more of him for twenty years. He did not, however, lose his early "glow," as alas! do so many; for when Paul and his companions came to Caesarea during the apostle's journey to Jerusalem preceding his arrest, they "entered into the house of Philip . . . and abode there" (Acts 21: 8). The significant fact is, that Philip was there known as "the evangelist"—still the devoted, zealous, self-effacing servant of God and winner of souls, as in his youth. And he who had witnessed abroad, far and wide, for his Lord, had commended Him also in his own home, to such effect that his four daughters were all engaged in the Master's service (v. 9). Happy is the preacher who sees his children not only growing up in the nurture and admonition of the Lord, but becoming in their turn Spirit-filled witnesses unto Him. That is the truest seal of any man's ministry—and his supreme joy.

So Philip continued unto the end. Legend gives differing accounts of his subsequent sphere of service, when persecution drove the Christians from Caesarea as it had driven them from Jerusalem long before: but we are not concerned with legend, and are content to close with the final glimpse we have of him in the Scripture—acting as host to the one whom he had preceded as forerunner, the great apostle of the Gentiles, whose spirit and service must have been so akin to his own. If only we had a record of their talk together! They served God in their day and generation and appointed spheres: and we are called to follow in their train, in our day and generation and appointed spheres. May we do it as worthily as they did.

Barnabas: The " Son of Consolation "

I F we could change our name, which one would we choose?
Or if we knew that the leaders of the Church, guided by the
Holy Spirit, were about to give us a new name indicative of
our character and our Christian service, would we rejoice or
tremble? We should probably regard the prospect with
apprehension, lest the selected name be unflattering, on the one
hand, or else should set a standard for our lives we could not
hope unfailingly to maintain. But such a problem does not
trouble us: we pay little attention to names, using them simply
for purposes of identification and seldom heeding any meaning
they might have. In the East it was otherwise, in Biblical times:
names were carefully chosen to express the aspirations of
parents for their offspring, or to indicate the characteristics
of the bearer. Accordingly it was not uncommon for names to
be changed when the character was formed, or when some
dominating purpose imparted to life a distinctive quality or
bent. It is therefore not surprising that we frequently read in
Scripture of new names given to mark crises in careers, or to
convey the outstanding traits of character.

Such was the case with Joses, or Joseph—it is not quite
certain which was his original name—a Levite from Cyprus,
to whom the apostles gave the surname Barnabas, meaning
"son of consolation" (A.V.), or "son of exhortation" (R.V.):
both renderings are legitimate, and each presents an equally
attractive portrait of the man so designated (Acts 4: 36). On
receiving it, he must have wondered if he could live up to so
challenging a name; yet how his heart must have rejoiced to
realize that the apostles so regarded him, and had given him

such a name by inspiration of the Holy Spirit Himself! His subsequent story, told in the Acts, shows how fully he fulfilled the prophetic intimation of his new name, and manifested the grace of both a son of consolation and of exhortation.

He first appears on the Biblical scene in Acts 4, where we are told that he, "having land, sold it, and brought the money, and laid it at the apostles' feet" (v. 37). This was clearly a voluntary and spontaneous act, although in accord with the general practice of the Church in Jerusalem at that time: for "as many as were possessed of lands or houses sold them, and brought the prices . . . and laid them down at the apostles' feet" (vv. 34, 35). It was an expression of their wondrous sense of unity in the new life in Christ; of the realization of mutual dependence as members of the infant Church. Barnabas entered into this self-renouncing fellowship without hesitation or reservation, and in a spirit contrasting strongly with that of Ananias and Sapphira, whose sad story is told immediately afterwards. Possessions, and one's attitude toward them, are ever a sure test both of character and of consecration! In this first glimpse we have of Barnabas, we behold his large-hearted, self-effacing, utter devotion to the Lord and His Church.

It is as a "son of consolation"—the idiom "son of . . ." is characteristically Jewish, and signifies the principal traits of the person concerned—that we next meet Barnabas: for it was he who stood by the side of the newly-converted Saul of Tarsus when the Church of Jerusalem regarded him with suspicion (Acts 9: 26). The Church was not to be blamed for its cautious attitude, for Saul had indeed been a most bitter antagonist; and it was not at all improbable that such as he might pretend to be a convert, in order to obtain first-hand evidence on which to indict and condemn them. Their rebuff, however, might easily have stumbled the young convert, sensitive aristocrat that he was. But the embarrassing moment of suspicion and tension gave place to understanding and rejoicing as Barnabas played the part of a "son of consolation" indeed, and "declared . . . how he had seen the Lord in the way" (9: 27). It has been suggested that possibly he had known Saul previously; Cyprus was within the same province of the Roman Empire as Tarsus, Saul's home town; and they might even have been educated together. Whether that is so or not, he was quick to discern the sincerity of the new disciple, and ready to vouch for the reality of his faith in the Lord Jesus Christ.

It is a good thing to be sure of one's own faith; it is even better to be a strengthener and encourager of the faith of another. Such was the ministry of Barnabas to Saul. There can be little doubt that, whatever might have been the attitude of the Church toward him, Saul's faith would have remained steadfast, for it was already so firmly centred and fixed in Christ. But not all young converts are so; and the attitude toward them of other Christians, and of the Church in general, sometimes has incalculable effect. Many a wavering one has been brought into full fellowship with the Church through a kindly word of welcome; some, alas, are undoubtedly turned back by indifference or even aloofness on the part of those who should cherish them as lambs of Christ's flock. Henry Drummond once said, "How many prodigals are kept out of the Kingdom of God by the unlovely characters of those who profess to be inside!" Oh that there were more sons of consolation!

When the Jewish authorities realized that Saul was now converted to the "upstart" faith he had persecuted, they determined to kill him; so the Church in Jerusalem persuaded him to return to Tarsus. An interval of some years elapsed before he and Barnabas—who were destined to be so closely linked in missionary witness to the Gentiles—came together again. Once more Barnabas took an initiative which displayed the qualities expressed in his name.

Members of the Jerusalem Church, scattered abroad by the persecution which followed the martyrdom of Stephen, came to Antioch in Syria. There, they preached the Gospel to the "Grecians"—Jews born and reared outside Palestine, amid Greek culture and influences, and consequently more "liberal" in their outlook than those of Judæa—and "a great number believed, and turned to the Lord." Reports of this notable happening soon reached Jerusalem, and the "parent" Church

H

decided to send an emissary to supervise and encourage these new converts. For this delicate and highly responsible task Barnabas was selected: and no better choice could have been made. His gracious spirit, sound judgment and dedicated zeal fitted him to assess aright the events in Antioch, and also commended him to the infant Church there. The record in Scripture is brief but graphic. "When he came," says the Book of Acts, "and had seen the grace of God (Barnabas) was glad, and exhorted them all, that with purpose of heart they would cleave unto the Lord. For he was a good man," the record adds, "and full of the Holy Ghost and of faith" (11: 23, 24). Could a higher tribute than that be paid to any man?

Barnabas recognized the work of the Holy Spirit for what it was, and rejoiced in it; and he encouraged the new converts to steadfast continuance in the faith. He sounded forth the authentic note of true evangelism: that salvation is the gift of God to those who "with purpose of heart . . . cleave unto the Lord." All too often this essential element of the Gospel message is neglected, and the initial decision stressed almost to the point of implying that receiving Christ as Saviour is all that matters. The deliberate act of submission, the responding "Yes" of the heart to the Gospel invitation, the receiving of the Lord Jesus Christ as Saviour, is indeed crucially important: but this is only the beginning of a life in which there must be a cleaving unto the Lord with purpose of heart. By thus preaching the whole Gospel to this virile young Church at Antioch, Barnabas proved himself not only a son of consolation, but also a worthy "son of exhortation." No wonder the Church grew so sturdily, and became the centre of widespread evangelism.

Indeed, the rapid growth of the Church made it necessary for Barnabas to seek help in its oversight, and his thoughts turned to Saul. Accordingly he left for Tarsus to seek him—and the word implies that he had to search, for Saul had probably been disowned by his family (Phil. 3: 8) and was living—and witnessing, we are sure—elsewhere. Barnabas found him, however, and brought him to Antioch: and there the two engaged together in fruitful ministry (Acts 11 : 25, 26). When the Church wished to send a gift to "the brethren which dwelt in Judæa" stricken by famine, they "sent it by the hands of Barnabas and Saul" (v. 30): and it was probably during this visit to Jerusalem that the incident recorded in Galatians 2: 1–10 took place.

On their return to Antioch, "as they ministered to the Lord, and fasted, the Holy Spirit said, Separate me Barnabas and Saul for the work whereunto I have called them . . ." (Acts 13: 2). Thus the intrepid pair went forth upon what is usually termed Paul's first missionary journey: and it is significant that they began with a visit to Cyprus, the home of Barnabas. He appreciated the spiritual principle enshrined in our Lord's great commission, "go ye . . . *beginning at Jerusalem*," and to him, that meant his native island and home town or village. Yet the responsibility and privilege of making Christ known among his own people did not limit his horizon: this was only the beginning of the task, for the Lord's commission reached out "unto all the world." And Barnabas was ready to go wherever his Master might appoint.

In the early stages of their journey a subtle change of relationship between the two friends took place. The older man—senior in years most probably, as well as in Christian discipleship—had hitherto taken the leading part in their joint activities; it was truly a case of "Barnabas and Saul." But now the order was reversed, and henceforward we read of "Paul and Barnabas"—with the one notable exception of their further visit to Jerusalem, where Barnabas again naturally took the foremost place as spokesman, in presenting their "report" to the apostles (Acts 15: 12). Now, it must have been a supreme test of Christian grace, for the one who had been a "father in the faith" to his colleague, to recognize in the younger man gifts which marked him out as the leader in this great enterprise, and himself to accept whole-heartedly the secondary place. No less noble a man than Barnabas could have submitted to this reversal of their rôles, and completed the journey in such wondrous fellowship and effectual ministry.

It is sad indeed to read, after this record of brotherly companionship in such adventurous service for the Lord, that they quarrelled, and so bitterly as to cause irreparable separation. Even this, however, was due to the very qualities of their differing natures. The occasion was the desire of Barnabas to take his younger cousin, John Mark, with them on their proposed second journey; but Paul flatly refused to allow Mark to accompany them, because he had turned back during the first journey (Acts 15: 37, 38; *cf.* 13: 13). Argument has persisted all through the subsequent centuries as to which of the apostles—for so were both Barnabas and Paul designated from the beginning of their missionary journey (Acts 14: 4, 14, etc.)— was right: the truth is that both stood firm for what they regarded as a vital principle. Each of them had the limitations as well as the strength of his qualities; and each was, after all, human and therefore liable to err. Paul demanded nothing less than an utter dedication to the will of God which would never falter or look back. Such was the quality of his own dedication: and he required it in others. One manifestation of weakness on the part of Mark stamped him, in Paul's eyes, as unfitted for missionary service. Paul had the iron will and inflexible spirit of the true missionary pioneer, and was perhaps somewhat intolerant of those cast in less heroic mould. Barnabas, while as dauntless and devoted as Saul, yet had a more sympathetic understanding of his kinsman's human frailty, and of his undoubted repentance concerning his failure; he was ready to give Mark a second chance, persuaded that this time he would make good. The two views were irreconcilable: and who shall say which was right?

One lesson at least we can learn from this sad incident: that even our profoundest convictions are not infallible. We must, of course, be true to those convictions; but we err in regarding them as the only possible expression of the will of God in the matter concerned. To us, the issue is so clear, it seems that those holding other views are controverting the truth; but they may be as sincere in their convictions as we are in ours, and have as good Scriptural and spiritual grounds for them. Few of us can comprehend all the truth of any circumstances or situation: we see and judge in part. While adhering to our convictions, however, we should never seek to impose them on others as the only possible correct interpretation of facts and events, and the sole expression of God's will. Paul and Barnabas both saw clearly *certain aspects* of the case in dispute; and none of us has the right to act as judge between them, as to which was nearer the mind of Christ. Certainly it seems that the Church in Antioch agreed with Paul (15: 40); and certainly also Barnabas disappears from the record at this point. We are told only that he took Mark and sailed into Cyprus, and after that we know no more. Tradition has much to say about him, but it is unreliable; and the apocryphal gospel and epistle of Barnabas are both manifestly of a later date.

For us the lessons of his life are manifold: and his example is an inspiration to all who regard it prayerfully. And even from its final recorded episode we can learn that the most saintly are yet human: we all have the treasure of divine grace in earthen vessels. Even so, we may serve our day and generation in the will of God, to His glory and the extension of His Kingdom.

Paul, too, had the limitations as well as the strength of his character; and his subsequent references to Mark seem to imply a regret for his severe opinion, and to express a half-apology (Col. 4: 10; 2 Tim. 4: 11). Unmitigated, his severity might have crushed the spirit of the weaker man, whereas the consolation extended to him by Barnabas strengthened his resolve to live down his failure, and to prove himself a worthy companion of apostles: which he did (see above; and Philemon 24; 1 Pet. 5: 13). Is it too much to infer that Paul came to think that Barnabas had been right, after all? Did he realize that, while we can never set too high a standard of discipleship for our own lives, yet toward others it is better to fulfil the ministry of a "son of consolation" than it is to condemn? Our Lord, looking upon faulty, needy, wayward men, was "moved with compassion:" and His disciples are most Christ-like when they are most compassionate. And *that* was the governing quality of the life of Barnabas. To the end, then, Barnabas was true to his name: he lived out the prophetic intimation of the delightful "Christian surname" bestowed on him by the Spirit of God through the apostles.

Two other references complete the New Testament portrait of Barnabas. The first is the indication that, like Paul, he received no support from the churches, but kept himself by the labour of his hands (1 Cor. 9: 6); and the second, Paul's revealing comment that, when Peter at Antioch separated himself from the Gentiles through the fear of "them of the circumcision," other Jewish Christians dissembled likewise, "insomuch that Barnabas also was carried away with their dissimulation" (Gal. 2: 13). A wealth of significance lies in that phrase, which can be rendered "*even* Barnabas. . . ." It reveals an esteem for Barnabas, on the part of Paul, surpassing that which he had for Peter! Despite the cleavage which had come between them, Paul still loved him and knew him to be a great and true man of God. "Even Barnabas . . ." Is there not a tenderness, a respect, a yearning in the phrase, which forms a fitting epitaph to one of the brightest "lesser lights" in the firmament of the Word? Perhaps this phrase, indeed, is an equal tribute to the man who wrote it, and him of whom he wrote. It reveals the greatness and Christ-likeness of both men. Barnabas and Paul were at heart companions to the end, and worthy fellow-labourers with their Lord.

20

Silas: Companion of Paul the Missionary

I T is never easy to be the companion of a man of outstanding
gifts. Inevitably the colleague is overshadowed by the more
dominating personality, and must be content to "play
second fiddle," while on the other hand he must possess
qualities approaching those of his more gifted master or friend,
else he cannot be a true collaborator. In fact, few endowed with
the ability to be real companions to men of genius are content to
play that part. Consequently, those of brilliant intellect are
often lonely people; either surrounded by inferior sycophants,
or associates with whom they incessantly quarrel!

That is natural enough. But the glory of the Gospel lies in
the fact that grace triumphs over natural inclinations and
proclivities. Saul of Tarsus, come to the full stature of his
remarkable abilities, would have been an angular person to
serve. But Paul the apostle was blessed with companions in his
missionary journeyings, whose loyal friendship reflects as much
to his credit as to theirs—and still more, to the grace of God in
all concerned. One of the most notable of these associates was
Silas.

Silas was under no illusion regarding the task he was undertaking, for the suggestion that he should accompany Paul on his
second missionary journey arose out of the apostle's rupture
with Barnabas. If Paul had quarrelled with that gracious and
peaceable man, he could be no complaisant personality! But
Silas readily consented to go with him, assured that the call
was in accord with the will of God: and how worthy a helper of
the great apostle to the Gentiles he proved to be! In deliberate
self-effacement he, one of the "chief men among the brethren"

in the Church in Jerusalem (Acts 15: 22) became a subordinate colleague of a "lone wolf" whom some in that Church regarded with suspicion and reserve. He journeyed and toiled, preached and suffered with the apostle; and shared with him the joy of instructing and strengthening the infant Churches in Asia Minor, and of pioneer evangelism in Europe. The story of their ordeal at Philippi is one of the epics of the Acts.

Yet, much as we read of him, we have not one recorded word that he spoke. This is remarkable, for Silas was no mere travelling companion, content to leave the preaching entirely to Paul. Indeed, one of the first things we learn of him is that he was a prophet (Acts 15: 32); and there is frequent reference to his preaching—but no single sentence that he uttered has come down to us. Despite this lack, however, we have a clear pen-portrait of the man: and we behold in him a fearless, noble-hearted servant of Christ and missionary of the Gospel.

Tradition has it that he was one of the "seventy" sent out by our Lord to witness two by two: and this is widely accepted, though we have no proof of it. We do not know how he became a disciple of Christ: he is introduced to us in the book of Acts in the story of the Council at Jerusalem, which was convened to discuss and settle the dispute regarding the relationship of Gentile converts to the Levitical law. Certain Jewish Christians from Jerusalem had caused dissension in Antioch by asserting that Gentile converts must become adherents of the Jewish faith, if they would enter into the true blessedness of the Gospel; for Christianity, they declared, was but the full-flowering of Judaism. Paul and Barnabas resisted these legalizers, and in order to secure an official declaration on the matter from the apostles in Jerusalem, went there to present the case (Acts 15). After lengthy consideration, under the chairmanship of James, the brother of our Lord, the Council set forth in writing its "charter of liberty" for Gentile converts, from the bondage of the law. In order to attest and endorse the authority of this document, the Jerusalem Church sent two of its own "chief men," Silas and Judas surnamed Barsabas; these accompanied

Paul and Barnabas back to Antioch, where they "exhorted the brethren with many words, and comforted them."

Thus we see Silas vested with authority as a delegate of the Jerusalem Church, in addition to his prestige as a recognized "prophet." Yet this distinguished and honoured Church leader was prepared to become the assistant of one with somewhat ambiguous standing in the Church, at the call of God. Here was a response akin to that of Isaiah long before, "Here am I; send me," such as we witness all too seldom today. Personal considerations were set aside in order that he might fulfil the revealed will of God for his life and service. Incidentally, Silas had a further valuable qualification for this missionary enterprize: apparently he, like Paul, was a Roman citizen (Acts 16: 37, 38), and so the awkward predicament could not arise of Paul being able to claim privileges which his companion was denied.

The narrative of their journeyings makes quite clear that Silas took his full part in all that was involved in their joint ministry—in the toiling, preaching, teaching and personal witness. Their absolute oneness of heart and mind, their comparable courage and zest, their equally devoted love to the Lord, is exemplified in the story of their experience at Philippi. Both men were unceremoniously stripped and severely beaten, and afterwards thrust into the noxious inner prison, with their feet fast in the stocks. But at midnight "Paul and Silas prayed and sang praises unto God." Our hearts never fail to glow as we read yet again the familiar record of their sublime courage and faith, in such circumstances. We could expect it of Paul; but Silas was his compeer in this glorious triumph of the spirit. It is one thing to keep pace with such as Paul in the normal course of his life; but to rise to the supreme heights of apostolic grace and testimony, is an accomplishment which distinguishes Silas as a man of equal faith and fortitude and devotion to his Lord as Paul himself. No wonder they worked and witnessed together so harmoniously, and to such good effect.

This incident, with its equally notable sequel in the conversion of the jailor—in which, also, Silas took his full part—

marked the peak of their joint experiences. Silas continued
with Paul in his itinerary to Thessalonica, and on to Berea;
there, the apostle was hustled out of the city by the disciples
because of threatening uproar, and he proceeded to Athens,
alone. Silas and Timothy (who had accompanied them from
Derbe to Philippi, and rejoined them at Berea) brought gifts
from the Macedonian Churches to Paul, when they met him
later, by arrangement, at Corinth (18: 5). Here Paul stayed for
eighteen months; and here the partnership with Silas ended. We
are not told how the separation came about; Silas just disappears from the narrative. Quite probably he felt that his
mission was completed, when it seemed that Paul was settling
down to pastoral work. He was no longer needed, as when
they were travelling from place to place, and felt constrained
to return to his home and his own Church in Jerusalem.

Silas is undoubtedly the Silvanus—the Roman form of the
name—whom Paul associates with himself and Timothy in the
opening salutations of the second epistle to the Corinthians and
the two epistles to the Thessalonians. He is also almost
certainly the Silvanus whom Peter describes, in his epistle "to
the strangers scattered throughout Pontus, Galatia, Cappadocia,
Asia and Bithynia"—in parts at least of which Silas had
ministered—as "a faithful brother unto you" (1 Pet. 5: 12).
That indeed is a worthy summing up of his character. "Brother,"
invested with its Christian significance, is an eloquent word, and
one exemplified in Silas. But that is not all: he was, Peter
testifies, a *faithful* brother—faithful to the Lord, in the trust
committed unto him; and faithful to those on whose behalf he
had received his King's commission. "Faithful" is one of the
noble adjectives applied to our Lord Himself, in His grace
toward mankind; and in conferring it upon Silas, the apostle
was witnessing to his loyal discipleship and likeness to his Lord.

21

Epaphras and Epaphroditus: Messengers to Paul the Prisoner

I T is striking that the only two official representatives of Churches to Paul during his first imprisonment in Rome, so far as we know, bore the same name—for Epaphras is but a contraction of Epaphroditus. Epaphras came from Colosse and Epaphroditus from Philippi, both bringing messages of Christian fellowship and encouragement from the Churches they represented, and Epaphroditus also laden with gifts, in practical expression of the concern and love of the Philippians for the apostle. Some Bible students have suggested that Epaphras and Epaphroditus were in fact one and the same person; but it is generally agreed that the two were quite distinct: Epaphroditus was a very common name, in both its full and contracted forms. Opinion differs also concerning the chronological order of their visits: Lightfoot and Moule are among the minority who think that Epaphroditus came from Philippi soon after the apostle's arrival in Rome, and that Epaphras followed some time later. The great majority, however, agree with tradition in reversing this order; and that is the sequence we shall assume to be correct.

Epaphras was seemingly a native of Colosse (Col. 4: 12) whose great privilege it had been to bring the Gospel to his fellow-citizens. Paul speaks of him as his own delegate, so manifestly he had become a Christian through the apostle's ministry elsewhere—probably at Ephesus, during the two years in which "all they which dwelt in Asia heard the word of the Lord Jesus" (Acts 19: 10). Wishing to devote his life to the service of his new-found Lord, he was sent back by Paul to Colosse, to make

Christ known among his family and friends and neighbours.
And God had honoured the faithful preaching of His word—
and not only in Colosse; for Epaphras was apparently the
pioneer evangelist to Laodicea and Hierapolis also (Col. 4: 13).
Under his leadership and pastoral care a strong Church was
established and built up in Colosse. He had been careful to
emphasize, however, that he was himself dependent upon Paul
for instruction and guidance: hence the note of authority in
Paul's Epistle to the Church, even while acknowledging that he
had never met them face to face (2: 1). Their concern at Paul's
arrest in Jerusalem and subsequent confinement in Caesarea—
of which they would in due course hear—must have been profound; and when he was taken to Rome in order to appear
before Caesar, they lost no time in sending assurance of prayerful thought and goodwill (1: 7, 8). Who was a better messenger
than Epaphras himself? The renewal of personal contact with
the apostle would be the greatest comfort and joy to him; and
no one could more fittingly express their love and solicitude.

Epaphras had another reason also for wishing to visit Paul,
more compelling even than the messages he carried: for his
soul was deeply distressed by a strange heresy which had taken
root in the Church. Known as "the Colossian heresy," it has
been the subject of much speculation, and is generally assumed
to have been a mixture of Judaistic legalism with the fantastical
beliefs of an incipient gnosticism. Epaphras had been unable to
stem the tide of this intrusive error, and hastened to the apostle
at the first opportunity, to consult with him.

In his Epistle to the Church—written while Epaphras was
still with him at Rome—Paul seeks not only to refute the error,
but also to reinforce the position and prestige of Epaphras, to
whom they owed their knowledge of the Gospel. In emphasizing the close relationship between Epaphras and himself, Paul
describes him as "my dear fellow-servant, who is for you (or
rather, 'in our behalf') a faithful minister of Christ" (1: 7);
and in the salutation he uses the still stronger term "a servant
—literally, slave—of Christ" (4: 12). Now this word, expressive
of absolute dedication to the Lord, Paul claims for himself—as

do Peter and James and Jude in their Epistles; but he never applies it to others, with two solitary exceptions—once to Timothy (Phil. 1: 1), and here to Epaphras. It signifies an exceptional degree of devotion to Christ and His service.

A most interesting problem is posed by Paul's further reference to Epaphras, in the Epistle to Philemon (v. 23), as "my fellow-prisoner in Jesus Christ." Now in the Epistle to the Colossians, Aristarchus is thus described, and Epaphras "my fellow-servant"; but in Philemon these terms are reversed. This has led to the suggestion that the companions of Paul took it in turns voluntarily to share his confinement. This may have been the case; but if not, and Epaphras was literally a prisoner, then almost certainly it was a result of his devotion to the apostle.

However it came about, the fact that he was the apostle's "fellow-prisoner" prevented Epaphras from returning to Colosse with this Epistle and that to Philemon (for the two were sent together). Distance did not dim his concern for his "flock," however. "I bear him record," says the apostle, "that he hath a great zeal for you." But how could a man express "great zeal" for the Church from which he was separated by a great distance? The apostle explains: "always labouring fervently for you in prayers, that ye may stand perfect and complete in all the will of God." And that, says Alexander McLaren, is "the noblest service which Christian love can do . . . Love has no higher way of utterance than prayer."

Much is said and written about prayer, yet few Christians really pray. Oh yes, we, mention a few names in our daily intercessions: but striving in prayer for others—as Abram did for Sodom, Moses for the rebellious children of Israel, Daniel for his nation, and Paul also, for his brethren according to the flesh: what do most of us know of prayer like this? Let Epaphras be our pattern. His prayers were offered, not merely for his family and personal friends; they were not even limited to his own Church at Colosse, but embraced also the sister Churches of Laodicea and Hierapolis. True prayer is the most self-effacing exercise possible to man. It can only be sustained by deep and unfeigned love. For prayer of value is costly, involving both travail of soul and expenditure of time. A casual "God bless So-and-so" is not prayer according to the Biblical pattern. "Pray without ceasing," Paul exhorted the Thessalonians; and Epaphras exemplified that exhortation by "always labouring fervently . . . in prayer."

Now, strong as is the expression "labouring fervently," it still falls short of conveying the force of the original, which is literally "wrestling in agony." Two Biblical scenes are recalled vividly to mind by that graphic phrase—the wrestling of the patriarch Jacob, by which he earned a new name, Israel, and entered into a new life of fellowship with God; and more sacred still, the agony of our Lord in the garden.

It seems almost presumptious to consider our praying in relation to the life-transforming wrestling of Jacob at Jabbok, and—inestimably more so—to the agony of Jesus in Gethsemane. Yet that is just the setting in which the apostle deliberately places the prayer-life of Epaphras, and through him, of us all. Laying hold upon God with an intensity of purpose which will not let Him go until he blesses; striving even unto agony of spirit, that His will may be done: no wonder Alexander McLaren declares that Epaphras was "a type of the highest service that love can render." And no wonder Paul accorded him the designation expressing the loftiest conception of discipleship: "a bondslave of Jesus Christ." The word "bondslave," most hated and despised in the Roman world, became the title of highest honour in the Kingdom of God. It indicates supremely the inner secret of prevailing prayer.

Inevitably, as effect from cause, such an one as Epaphras was "a faithful minister of Jesus Christ"—and than that, no higher tribute can be paid to any pastor. Disappointments and travail he may have; seemingly his work may be spoiled and his flock deluded: but "it is required in a steward that a man be found faithful" (1 Cor 4: 2). And Epaphras has that glorious encomium.

Epaphroditus was apparently, unlike Epaphras, not a leader but just one of the members of the Church at Philippi, chosen for this mission to Paul because of his zealous desire to be of service to his fellow-believers and to the apostle. There was an especially close bond between Paul and the Philippians: of all the Churches which he founded, they remained the most grateful and devoted. As he records in his Epistle to them, they had on several occasions sent practical tokens of their love and prayerful fellowship during his missionary journeyings, until he travelled too far afield, and later was arrested. So, for some years, they "lacked opportunity" to show their esteem for him in this way: but on learning that he was in Rome, they once more sent greetings and gifts.

The joy of Epaphroditus in fulfilling this commission can easily be imagined: and he was not content merely to convey the messages and bestow the goods he carried to meet the apostle's necessities. There is a more intimate and more precious expression of love than the most kindly words or the most appropriate gifts can convey—the rendering of personal service: and that also, Epaphroditus supplied. "He ministered to my wants," said the apostle; co-operating so whole-heartedly in the various activities in which Paul was engaged despite his incarceration, that he literally worked himself almost to death. Some commentators suggest that he probably caught the fever prevalent at Rome, but Paul explicitly states that it was "for the work of Christ" that Epaphroditus was "nigh unto death"—so much so that his recovery was regarded by the apostle as an intervention of God, in answer to earnest prayer. It is noteworthy that Paul had no permanent powers of miraculous healing, but in this emergency could only commit his friend to the grace of God in prayer, as we might do today.

Raised up by God, Epaphroditus naturally longed to return home—especially so as he thought his friends would hear of his illness and be worried about him. What a tender heart he had for the welfare of others! His overflowing kindliness and readiness to do good had led him to undertake the arduous journey to Rome, and there to minister so devotedly to the apostle; and in that same considerate thought for others, he now yearned to return to his fellow-believers at Philippi, to set their minds at rest concerning him. So Paul sent him home again, with the "Epistle to the Philippians."

In recording his heartfelt appreciation of the fellowship of Epaphroditus, Paul describes him by three terms which, to-gether, present a composite picture of ideal Christian relation-ship—"my brother, and companion in labour, and fellow-soldier" (Phil. 2: 25). "Brother" is one of the many words invested with a new wealth of meaning by the Christian Gospel. It speaks of a most intimate relationship. Physically, the bond of brotherhood is close; but like all else associated with our fallen human nature, it has been marred by sin. A conse-quence of the fall was the uprising of hatred instead of love between brothers, so disastrously that the first murder was committed against a brother; and even the twin brothers Jacob and Esau became antagonists rather than boon companions. But in Christ "the sons of Adam boast more blessings than their father lost," and the ideal envisaged in the bond of brotherhood is restored. A kinship closer than that of blood is established between the members of the "household of God" (Ephes. 2: 19).

Our Lord declared the superiority of this new bond of spiritual relationship when, a message being brought that His mother and brethren desired to speak with Him, He asked, "Who is my mother? and who are my brethren?" and looking round upon His disciples He exclaimed, "Behold my mother and my brethren! For whosoever shall do the will of my Father which is in heaven, the same is my brother, and sister, and mother" (Matt. 12: 48, 50). And on the eve of His Passion He formally constituted the "household of faith" (Gal. 6: 10) when He said to the twelve, "With desire I have desired to eat this Passover with you before I suffer"—for the Passover was essentially a *family* festival: each family assembled to partake of it, as their forebears had done in Egypt. But Jesus deliberately departed from this custom, and by observing the Passover thus with the disciples, signified the establishing of a new family, of which He was the Head. The term "brother," then, as used by Paul, is no mere euphemism or figure of speech: it conveys a bond in which there is a knitting of heart with heart and spirit with spirit, in mutual faith and hope and love.

Such a fellowship between believers will inevitably lead on to companionship in service: for vital Christian faith must express itself in witness. This is life's greatest privilege: and it is realized in its fullness in "the fellowship of kindred minds." Its true quality and joy derive, of course, from the fact that thus we become, not only "companions in labour" one with another, but supremely "co-workers together with God." It is the presence and grace and power of the Lord that impart the value to both Christian fellowship and Christian service.

Christian graces go in threes, and so Paul completes his triad concerning Epaphroditus with "fellow-soldier." This follows as naturally upon "companions in labour" as that had followed "brother"; the three are inseparable aspects of this blessed relationship between true disciples.

This culminating characteristic introduces the note of *costliness* inevitable to effectual Christian service: a note soft-pedalled too often today, to the great weakening of the Church's vitality. The cause of Christ calls for the highest qualities and most exacting devotion. "Endure hardness as a good soldier of Jesus Christ," Paul exhorted Timothy; ready to toil and strive and endure; ready to go wherever commanded, to do and to dare and even to die. For a soldier is a man utterly dedicated to the service of his sovereign. Toil and travail, conflict and constant vigilance: these are the expected lot of the soldier. And shall we not spend and be spent, toil and fight and pray in the service of the King of kings?

All this Epaphroditus had been, and all this he had done, in his fellowship with Paul. Now the time had come for him to return home, bearing the apostle's letter of gratitude for all that the Church at Philippi had sent him—which, Paul said, was "an odour of a sweet smell, a sacrifice acceptable, well-pleasing to God." That is strong language to use concerning gifts of food and clothing and money, the necessities of everyday life: for these terms are elsewhere applied to exalted acts of worship ascribed to God Himself. But that is precisely what the apostle

I

declares the practical helpfulness of the Philippian Christians to be. Even more: in writing to the Ephesian Church he uses these very expressions concerning the self-dedication of Christ unto the death of the Cross: "an offering and a sacrifice to God for a sweet-smelling savour." In the practical expression of Christian love and fellowship one toward another, then, His people *worship God*, in a manner most precious and pleasing to Him, and in accord with the spirit and sacrifice of His Son. Not only in the singing of psalms and hymns, rendering "the fruit of our lips" in thanksgiving and adoration, but also in the work of our hands, in His name and for His sake, do we render spiritual sacrifices glorifying and gratifying to Him. That is why the writer to the Hebrews says, "To do good and to communicate forget not, for with such sacrifices God is well pleased."

And of that privileged service, Epaphroditus is a shining example.

22

Onesiphorus: A Friend in Need

A<small>LL</small> that we know of Onesiphorus is contained within three verses of Paul's second letter to Timothy (1: 16–18): but these are enough to present a pleasing portrait of a man who proved himself a true friend of the apostle at a time of desperate need. This brief passage has a further great interest, however, for Paul expresses his indebtedness to Onesiphorus in somewhat cryptic phrases which have been a focus of controversy throughout twenty centuries. It is impossible to separate the personality of Onesiphorus from the problem of prayers for the dead.

Paul was nearing the end of his remarkable career as "an apostle, and a teacher of the Gentiles" (1: 11): he knew that he had finished his course, and that the time of his departure was at hand (4: 6–7). In this farewell letter to his beloved "son" Timothy, he recounts rather wistfully that "all they which are in Asia be turned away from me; of whom are Phygellus and Hermogenes"—from whom apparently he might have expected loyal devotion to the end. In contrast to their defection, the unwavering friendship of Onesiphorus shines out in brighter splendour. For "he oft refreshed me, and was not ashamed of my chain."

There lies the supreme test, by which Onesiphorus was proven a worthy friend of the apostle, while all others of Asia were shown to be but "fair-weather friends." For Paul was under sentence of death; and to be known as an acquaintance of a condemned Christian in Nero's Rome was to incur grave risk. The persecution of Christians was a popular pursuit, and those who valued their physical safety more than spiritual privileges, considered it expedient to dissociate themselves from so prominent a Church leader as Paul.

In these circumstances, to maintain contact with the apostle, to stand loyally with him, required a courage which few could command. Onesiphorus revealed yet higher qualities, however; for at such a time as this he *sought Paul out* "very diligently." Coming to Rome, probably on business, and recognizing the situation for what it was, he allowed no consideration of personal safety to deter him from discovering the whereabouts of the apostle—apparently at considerable effort. It would have been so easy to make excuses for not "running undue risk"; so easy to find it "impossible" to learn where Paul was detained. It meant inquiry—repeated inquiry; and of the very officials who were putting into effect Nero's policy of persecution of Christians. To seek Paul was to attract their attention, and invite disaster for oneself. Yet Onesiphorus counted not the cost, but "sought me out . . . and found me."

Having done that, this visitor to Rome from Ephesus showed that his friendship had the quality of endurance. "He oft refreshed me," Paul testifies of him; "and was not ashamed of my chain." Many had proffered their friendship during the apostle's early apprehension in Rome; but one after another they abandoned him as it became increasingly hazardous to be known as a Christian. Paul's wistful, unrecriminating comment makes sad reading: "Demas hath forsaken me. . . . At my first hearing no man stood with me, but all forsook me. . . ." Fortitude and the courage of undeviating faith were demanded for sustained friendship to Paul the prisoner. And those qualities Onesiphorus possessed and displayed. He not only "sought me out very diligently" but, says the apostle, he then "oft refreshed me"—without expectation of reward or commendation.

Many are spurred to an act of kindness by high ideals or noble resolutions; but it takes more than that to repeat the kindness, at considerable personal cost; and to keep on, so long as the need exists or circumstances allow. It is *continuance* in welldoing that presents the test and wins the crown (Gal. 6: 9; Col. 1: 23).

There was a more subtle influence than personal danger, however, deterring some from steadfast friendship to Paul. It is indicated in the special commendation of Onesiphorus in that he "was not ashamed of my chain." That would seem a small consideration beside the risk of torture and death. But is it? There are many who, if brought to the issue, would bravely face martyrdom for Christ's sake, who yet fail in the insidious testings summed up in the phrase "what people think." It is easier to die for Christ than it is to bear His reproach. There is no stigma in being the friend of Christians who enjoy as good or better social standing than ourselves; but only true godliness will befriend the despised and the desolate. We find it desirable to be intimate with those whose acquaintance enhances our pleasure and prestige; quite otherwise to associate with the lowly and outcast. In Paul's day, it was gratifying to be the friend of an apostle likely to regain his liberty and exercise authority in the Church; but quite a different matter when he was manacled and condemned—albeit by the very Power which crucified his Lord. It is by such considerations as these that the true nobility of the friendship of Onesiphorus can be assessed.

Different as are our circumstances today from those of Paul in Nero's Rome, this story of friendship has a most relevant present application. For the words "not ashamed" recur repeatedly in the epistles. In this very letter to Timothy, Paul refers to his condition as a condemned prisoner for Christ's sake, and adds in ringing tones, "Nevertheless I am not ashamed, for I know whom I have believed. . . ." Not ashamed to suffer, to be despised and condemned, for the sake of Him who—for our sakes—was despised and rejected of men. Years before, Paul had declared to the Romans, ere ever he saw their city, "I am not ashamed of the Gospel of Christ, for it is the power of God unto salvation. . . ."—the Gospel of the Cross, which to the Greeks is foolishness and to the Jews a stumbling-block; the Gospel which demands that we "go unto Him without the camp, bearing His reproach." Ashamed of the Gospel? Ashamed of Christ? Ashamed of any child and servant of His? There is only one thing of which we should be ashamed—that is, of being ashamed of *Him*, or *them*! And the glory of the Gospel is this: that our Lord, the Lord of glory, is *not ashamed to call us His brethren* (Heb. 2: 11); and God Himself is not ashamed to be called our God (11: 16).

Now this nobility of conduct on the part of Onesiphorus in Rome was in keeping with his character and manner of life in his home and among his neighbours. "In how many things he ministered at Ephesus thou knowest very well," writes Paul to Timothy—who was then in that city, exercising oversight of the Church, as the apostle's delegate. Of course, only a man habitually seeking the well-being of others, rather than his own, would display such self-forgetting, self-spending loyalty to a friend, in a far country. Men seldom rise in time of crisis above the level of their accepted standards. And it should be observed that the A.V. is misleading in its translation, "he ministered *unto me* . . ."—those two last words should be omitted as in the R.V. and other translations. His "ministry" was not limited to the apostle: the implication is that Onesiphorus was one who delighted in doing good—all the good he could, to whomsoever he could. It was not a case of partiality to an especial friend, but a consistent out-going of goodwill to others, expressed in practical kindly deeds. No wonder that he "oft refreshed" Paul in his hour of greatest need when, forsaken by others, and enduring rigorous imprisonment, he awaited his dread interview with the executioner.

We might wonder why it was that the apostle set so much store by the companionship of Onesiphorus: surely he had such an intimacy of fellowship with the Lord, such a realization of His presence and comforting grace, that he was independent of the support of earthly friends? Yes, it is true that, if need be, he could testify that the Lord was indeed his sufficiency. When all men forsook him, he could affirm that "notwithstanding the Lord stood with me, and strengthened me. . . ." Yet if our Lord Himself yearned for the companionship of the apostles in *His* hour of agony in the garden, how much more do even the greatest of His servants desire the consolation of a friendly

voice and comforting hand as they face life's final ordeal? That
was the service Onesiphorus rendered Paul. A deep and true
succour is expressed in the phrase "oft refreshed me"—for
while it conveys the implication of physical aid in the supply of
essentials and comforts, it also includes the much more
precious spiritual aids of fellowship and encouragement. So to
"refresh" another in the gravest hours and issues of life, is the
highest service anyone can render a friend.

How, then, does all this relate to the question of prayers for
the dead? In this: that Paul couches his entire reference to
Onesiphorus in terms which imply that he was dead, and in
words which the Church of Rome claim to be apostolic authority
and example for praying for the dead. "The Lord give mercy
unto the house of Onesiphorus," he says; and again, "The
Lord grant unto him that he may find mercy of the Lord in that
day." Now, it is not beyond dispute that he was in fact dead:
some commentators argue that, if he were, the apostle would
not have referred to "the house of Onesiphorus," as he does in
1: 16 and 4: 19. His family would no longer be "the house of
Onesiphorus" after his decease, they aver. But unbiased consideration of the passage makes the conclusion difficult to evade,
that he was dead. The comment concerning his "house"
presents no real difficulty: the apostle expresses the earnest hope
that the family of this good man might come, through faith in
Christ, to be numbered among the recipients of His "mercy"
in so-great salvation. In lively remembrance of the goodness of
Onesiphorus to him, Paul earnestly hopes and longs that his
family may, through the mercy of the Lord, be saved.

The reference to Onesiphorus himself, if he were dead, presents more difficulty. It is not a difficulty inherent in the text,
however, but simply that the Roman Church has pressed into it
a meaning which it manifestly does not possess. Here is a classic
example of the tendency—against which we all need constantly
to be on our guard—of reading into a text a significance we
wish it to possess in order to support our theories, rather than
educing from the Word its true, clear, simple meaning. For the
phrase, "The Lord grant unto him that he may find mercy

of the Lord in that day" can by no stretch of legitimate exegesis be reckoned as a prayer for the dead. Paul is plainly expressing something that he earnestly hopes will be the case: this is not a prayer, but a yearning desire concerning a beloved friend. The words "find mercy" might be rendered "find favour," and some expositors take them to mean, "be suitably rewarded"—for his goodness to Paul. The phrase is, however, identical with that concerning his "house" and seems to strike the deeper note conveyed by the A.V. rendering, "find mercy."

This leads to the question, Why, if Onesiphorus were such a good and loyal friend of the apostle, should Paul *hope* that, "in that day," he will be found among the redeemed? The conclusion is inescapable that, good man as he was, true friend of the apostle as he was, Paul was not absolutely sure that he was converted. He earnestly hoped so; but he could not confidently assert that Onesiphorus was among the great and glorious company before the throne of God and the Lamb.

How many there are today associated with our churches, of whom we could not be sure! Good people, often putting to shame by their quality of life those who make profession of consecration and godliness. Yet somehow they lack the confession of personal faith in Christ as Saviour; and who can say assuredly whether or not they are saved? Moreover, do not most of us earnestly trust that certain of our relatives and friends, now dead, are "with the Lord": we have ground for hope that they are, but we cannot confidently assert so. Have we never used concerning them just such a phrase as this: "The Lord grant that he may find mercy of the Lord in that day"?

Three pertinent and very practical lessons ensue: first, that salvation cannot be won by any quality of character we might manifest or any good deeds we may perform. If any man could *earn* his way to heaven, surely Onesiphorus would have done so by his devoted service to the apostle—and Paul would have been aware of the fact. But salvation is "not by works of righteousness which we have done, but according to His mercy . . . by the washing of regeneration, and renewing of the Holy

Ghost . . ." Much as Paul longed that Onesiphorus might share with him the glory and rejoicing of the saints in light, he *could not be sure*: even the apostle could do no more than express a yearning hope.

Again, intimacy with the people of God—even, in the case of Onesiphorus, with an apostle—is no substitute for relationship to the Lord. To trust Him as Saviour and Lord is the one thing supremely needful.

Then, most urgently, follows the lesson: that it is vitally important to "make our calling and election sure." We never know when the day of opportunity may close—as it apparently did in untimely fashion with Onesiphorus. But there is no need to be in doubt regarding our eternal destiny, or to leave others in doubt concerning us. The apostle could say for himself, "I know whom I have believed," and therefore to be "absent from the body" was to be "present with the Lord." No element of questioning or dubiety enters into his anticipation of his own future: "the time of my departure is at hand," he writes in this very epistle; "henceforth there is laid up for me a crown of righteousness, which the Lord, the righteous judge, shall give me at that day." And lest it be thought that only such as the apostle can have such confidence, he adds, "and not to me only, but unto all them also that love His appearing."

Don't remain in doubt. Don't leave any wistful questioning in the minds of others, concerning you. Make your calling and election *sure*, through a simple act of faith in Christ as your own Saviour and Lord.

23

Demas : And Others Whose Light Flickered

How reassuring it is that God's thoughts, and His ways, are not as ours. We are prone to dismiss with contempt those who stumble and fall. The Bible never condones such lapses, nor minimizes their consequences: but it reveals a love in God reaching far beyond the most enduring human affection; a grace and power to save when the most tolerant of men would consider the case utterly hopeless. "There's a wideness in His mercy like the wideness of the sea," affirmed F. W. Faber. It ill becomes us, then, to say of any man that his light flickered *out*; for the gallery of heroes of faith in Hebrews 11 contains some whose names we would consider more shameful than glorious. Who of us, for instance, would have included Samson, so self-indulgent despite remarkable experience of the divine grace, that he seemed to have forfeited all right to be regarded as a man of God? His New Testament counterpart is Demas, who "loved this present world."

Demas presents us with the problem of the paradoxical aspects of the teaching of Scripture, which has occasioned disputation from the earliest days of the Church's history. Can a Christian fall from grace and become lost? Some stern admonitions in the Word would seem to imply so, while other passages assure us of the eternal security of those who truly believe in the Lord Jesus Christ as their Saviour. The warnings are given that none should presume; the assurances, that no child of God should fear eternal separation from Him through a lapse of faith or conduct. But we must not think that we can resolve these great problems with a formula. Judgment belongs unto God; and we must await the answer to many perplexing questions until we know as we are known.

Demas, then, remains enigmatical in his character and destiny. Whether or not he was truly a Christian, we cannot dogmatically assert. The fact that he was a "fellow-labourer" with the apostle for a time (Philemon 24) does not decide the question: for Judas was an intimate companion and chosen apostle of our Lord Himself, yet became the traitor, and "went to his own place." Demas was, however, among the "inner circle" of Paul's friends during his first imprisonment at Rome; and he seems to have been known to the Church at Colosse and to Philemon, since his name is included in the salutations of the letters addressed to them. Commentators observe, however, that his name alone in the greetings to Colosse appears without any commendatory remark, and it is suggested that perhaps he already revealed the weakness which later proved to be his undoing. But what opportunity, what privilege was his! To be the companion of Paul, albeit under the constraints of the apostle's imprisonment; to have the benefits of his instruction and the inspiration of his unquenchable zeal—surely the faith of the most double-minded Christian would become unshakably rooted and grounded in such a favourable atmosphere? Alas, it is not inevitably so. The love of the world is so insidious an evil that not even apostolic example and counsel could subdue it.

Among the many speculations based upon Paul's restrained comment that "Demas hath forsaken me, having loved this present world" (2 Tim. 4: 10), two possible interpretations command widest support. One is, that Demas was never really a Christian, although attracted by the Gospel and its messenger. According to this view, personal ambition was his primary motive in attaching himself to the apostle. He thought that Paul would soon be released, and that friendship with him would secure for his companions position and prestige within the fast-growing Church. When Nero became Emperor, however, and the apostle lay under sentence of death, Demas realized that his hopes were in vain, and so went off to seek worldly advantage elsewhere. Reluctant as we may be to take so cynical a view of

Demas as this, it must be confessed that countless numbers have become professing Christians, and have sought office within the Church, for no higher motives. The "love of this present world" is a terrible thing when it invades the very fellowship of the redeemed!

A more charitable view is, that Demas unfeignedly embraced the Gospel message and at first joyously associated himself with its messenger, even though this meant the sharing of his privations and suffering. But after a while the early glow wore off; he began to cast regretful glances toward the life he had renounced; the comforts and circle of friends he had abandoned for Christ's sake. To do that is to invite disaster. The lure of the world is so powerful that any Christian who repeats the folly of Lot's wife and looks back, places himself in direst peril. "Love not the world, neither the things that are in the world," urged the aged apostle John, well knowing its insidious attraction and its destructive power: "If any man love the world, the love of the Father is not in him." And our Lord Himself said that "No man, having put his hand to the plough, and looking back, is fit for the Kingdom of God." Such an one exemplifies the seed sown among thorns, in our Lord's parable (Matt. 13: 7, 22).

Did Demas abandon his faith, as well as forsake the apostle? Tradition avers that he did: but it speaks with unreliable voice. We cannot evade the fact, however, that in this last glimpse we have of him in Scripture, his back is turned to the people of God and his hands are stretched out to grasp what this world— this present evil age—has to offer. His story gives warning against double-mindedness, which inevitably leads to the betrayal of the best for the transitory and the trivial. If he were indeed converted, then his soul was saved eternally, "yet so as by fire." But his name has been associated through all the centuries of Church history with the ignominy of back-sliding and of the forsaking of the apostle in his hour of deepest need. We can only hope that, like Samson, he renewed at the last the vows he had violated, and found a place of repentance and restoration. Even so, the opportunities he lost were lost beyond recall. Our Lord's words concerning His own ministry set the

highest standard, and present the most solemn warning—
"I must work the works of Him that sent me while it is day:
the night cometh when no man can work."

It might seem strange to include the story of Demas among the
illustrious records of faithful "lesser lights"; but in some
Scripture references he takes his place among such true saints
and servants of God. For a time he seemed to be a hero of the
faith; and his story is a salutary reminder that *time is the test*:
"he that endureth to the end shall be saved." Alas, the Bible
contains the record of several who, like Demas, began promis-
ingly, and then failed to fulfil that early promise. "Ye did run
well," Paul wrote to the Galatians: "who did hinder you?"

Perhaps even more pertinent to the majority of Evangelical
Christians today, are the allusions to those who, while unshaken
in faith and loyal membership of the Church, yet mar their
service and witness for Christ by faults of character or temperament which should be subdued by the Spirit of grace indwelling
them. "I beseech Euodias, and beseech Syntyche, that they be
of the same mind in the Lord," wrote Paul, in his Epistle to the
Philippians (4: 2). Even in that Church which occasioned the
apostle the greatest satisfaction, there was the jarring note of
quarrelling "sisters." How many Churches have their Euodias
and Syntyche! As James bluntly observed, concerning this and
kindred sins of the tongue, "My brethren, these things ought
not so to be." How ashamed Euodias and Syntyche must
have felt as the apostle's letter was read aloud in the Church,
and every eye was turned toward them: how ashamed many
another will feel when the book of remembrance is read at the
judgment seat of Christ.

Euodias and Syntyche would probably have scorned Demas
for his open break with the Church; they would have deplored
the harm he did to the cause of Christ by his apostasy. They
little realized that they themselves did probably as much harm
as he, and gave as much occasion to the heathen to blaspheme.
For quarrelling Christians are a reproach to the Gospel, and
a stumbling-block to the unsaved. The Christian's light can
flicker even though he remains sound in doctrine and punctilious

in church attendance and even in so-called Christian service. Don't scorn Demas too severely until you have examined your own life!

There is a yet more serious possibility set before us in Scripture, for we read of those who, remaining within the professing Church, yet become enemies of the truth; deceiving themselves and others, they fulfil the very work of Satan. Heresy soon reared its ugly head in the early Church, and hindered the proclamation of the Gospel and checked the spiritual growth of the young Church, as much as did the forces of evil without. It is a solemn thought that the false teachers within the Church were as harmful in their influence as the hostile Jews and the resentful protagonists of heathen faiths. The tragedy of the majority of these false teachers lay in the fact that they persuaded themselves —and alas, others also—that *they* were the true believers, more enlightened than those who adhered to the "simple" apostolic Gospel. Such self-deception has characterized most of the propagators of error whose influence has rent the Church and led countless numbers away from the truth as it is in Jesus: and that fact constitutes the most solemn warning. The faith once for all delivered to the saints is revealed in the written Word, and clearly expressed, we believe, in the credal statements of the Reformed Church—perhaps the most lucid and faithful exposition of the fundamental verities ever formulated. Any departure from these, any claim of "new light" or especial revelation, is fraught with gravest possibilities of error. The safest principle is that expressed in the time-honoured maxim, "Keep to the middle of the King's highway." Then the light of faith and of witness will burn steadily and brightly, and be in no danger of flickering—much less of flickering out.

24

Titus, Tychicus and Trophimus:
Apostolic Delegates

A COMPARATIVELY few personalities dominate the story of the early Church as recorded in the New Testament, so that we are apt to think there were indeed only a handful of leaders and outstanding men. That manifestly would be a very mistaken view. While the spotlight focuses upon these few, as it were, many others make brief appearance in the drama who plainly possessed abilities of a high order, and a loyalty to the Lord Jesus Christ and His Gospel which found expression in devoted service.

Among the many fellow-labourers of the apostle Paul—to use his own term regarding them—priority of place must be given to his beloved "son" Timothy. In the ardours of his later missionary journeyings and in the rigours of his imprisonments, the undeviating attachment and zealous co-operation of the younger man was the apostle's greatest comfort and joy. There were, of course, some who shared his labours more fully, for a time, as nearer his equals in age and status: but these—such as Barnabas and Silas—for differing reasons parted company with him. From among his own converts, however, he gathered round him a group of ardent younger men who remained his companions and helpers to the end. It is heart-warming to read of the unflagging friendship they gave him through the protracted testings and ordeals of his imprisonments at Rome—even through the dark days when all in Asia forsook him. More important still: by their willingness to go anywhere and to undertake any task at his bidding, they enabled Paul to maintain and even to extend his ministry as the "apostle to the Gentiles" although he was in chains.

Timothy was too important a personage, as the apostle's most intimate friend and chief delegate to the various Churches, to be regarded as a "lesser light." Let it suffice to say that he exemplified the spirit of discipleship in his readiness to fulfil whatsoever service might be required of him, in the cause of Christ. It is generally thought that he was of delicate health and shy, retiring disposition; inclined to under-estimate his own abilities, and needing constant encouragement. If that were so his undertaking the commissions he did, at the apostle's behest, commands the greater respect. We should not assume too much, however, from the apostle's solicitude for him: Paul had all the tender concern of a father for Timothy. Indeed, the affection between them was so strong and deep, that we ought the more to admire their supreme devotion to the Lord Jesus Christ and His Kingdom, in that the apostle was ready to send Timothy, and he to go, upon protracted visits to Churches, to impart spiritual instruction and establish a stable Church order—when, had they considered their own inclinations, they would both have much preferred to remain together.

Almost as close to Paul as Timothy, and possibly providing more equal companionship, was Luke, "the beloved physician" —who as author of the third Gospel and of the Acts, also soars out of the category of the "lesser lights." We have occasional glimpses of quite a number, however, who served the apostle in very similar manner as did Timothy: and among these, Titus is the best known, because of the "pastoral epistle" which Paul wrote to him while he was fulfilling one of his "missions," in Crete. Actually, the references to Titus elsewhere in the New Testament are few, and he is not mentioned at all by name in the Acts—though there is an allusion to him in 15: 2. Titus was a Greek, and so, of course, uncircumcised; and when pressure was brought to bear upon the apostle, by the Jewish element within the Church, to circumcise his convert, he resolutely refused (Gal. 2: 1–5). This was a test-case of Gentile liberty in Christ; and the apostle, who soon afterwards circumcised

Timothy in order not to "stumble" the Jewish members of the Church (Acts 16: 3)—since Timothy was a half-Jew, having a Jewish mother—firmly refused to submit to the demand that Gentile converts should be subjected to the Jewish rite, and assume the yoke of the Law.

From his first appearance upon the scene, Titus was manifestly a trusted colleague of the apostle. During a period of great trouble within the Church of Corinth, occasioning Paul keen distress because of the dissensions, criticism of himself, and condoning of sin in their midst, Titus undertook the delicate mission of investigation and endeavour to bring order out of the chaos. It was a task demanding outstanding gifts of tact and spiritual authority. Some Bible students think that Timothy had already failed in just such a mission: but this is by no means certain. Titus was perhaps an older man than Timothy, possessing a more forceful character. However that may be, he dealt with the situation in such a way as to be able to bring back to the apostle a reassuring report: through his influence there was a righting of wrongs within the Church, and a repenting of sin. A bond of close relationship was established between Titus and the Corinthians, which was strengthened by subsequent visits—so much so that Paul says Titus shared with himself "the same earnest care" for the Church. He also describes Titus as his "brother" and "partner and fellow-helper concerning you" (2 Cor. 2: 13; 8: 23). In the Epistle to Titus, Paul addresses him as "mine own son." Those terms all express the warm affection of the apostle, his confidence in and esteem for Titus. Together with the especial relationship subsisting between spiritual "father" and "son" was the yet stronger bond of mutual regard and respect, as companions together in the work of the Lord.

The Epistle to Titus was written, most probably, during the period between the two imprisonments at Rome. Paul was approaching the end of his career, and had a longed-for opportunity of renewed personal evangelistic and pastoral ministry. But he was unable to go to all the places he wished to visit, and so continued to exercise his oversight of the Churches through those who might truly be called apostolic delegates—a term now impudently misapplied by the pontiff of the Roman Church to certain of his emissaries. Thus Titus was consolidating the work in Crete.

The last glimpse we have of him is given us in the apostle's final letter; and Titus is still engaged in missionary work under the apostle's authority, though now in Dalmatia (2 Tim. 4: 10). It is a blessed relationship indeed when men can work together in mutual faith and hope and love, strengthening and supporting one another in their differing yet complementary spheres and capacities; labouring together in the service of the hands, in spiritual counsel and in prayer. That is the Scriptural pattern of spiritual ministry.

Less is known of Tychicus and Trophimus, whose names are linked in Acts 20: 4 as "of Asia." We first meet them among Paul's companions on his fateful journey to Jerusalem: indeed, Trophimus was the unwitting occasion of the uproar which led to the apostle's arrest, for it was falsely rumoured that Paul—who was known to have Gentile friends—had taken a Gentile into the forbidden precincts of the Temple (Acts 21: 29).

What amount of contact his friends were able to maintain with the apostle in his imprisonments at Jerusalem and Caesarea we do not know; but both Tychicus and Trophimus appear later in the story. Tychicus followed Paul to Rome, and became the bearer of his letters to Ephesus and—with Onesimus —to Colosse. But he was more than a mere messenger: Paul writes of him to the Ephesians as "a beloved brother and faithful minister in the Lord"; and to the Colossians, "a beloved brother, and faithful minister and fellow-servant in the Lord, whom I have sent unto you . . . that he might know your estate and comfort your hearts." He was making a further visit to Ephesus at the time when Paul wrote his farewell letter to Timothy (4: 10); and Trophimus was ill at Miletum, where Paul had been obliged to leave him during the itinerary between the Rome imprisonments.

Thus we see all these, with others mentioned in 2 Timothy, loyal to the last, and untiring in the service of the apostle and of the Lord—theirs and his; whose bondslaves they delighted to account themselves. Who can doubt that they continued in such ministry after Paul's martyrdom, carrying on his work after he had gone to his reward. Thus the Church was strengthened and extended. As runners in a relay race hand on the torch to those who, in their turn, pass it on to yet others, so the message of the Gospel was carried to the bounds of the then known world—and handed on to succeeding generations, unto ourselves today. And those who received the torch from apostolic hands were Timothy and Titus and Tychicus, and countless others, named and unnamed in Holy Writ. Their debtors we are. We salute them, lesser lights maybe, but true torchbearers of the faith.

25

Paul's Portrait Gallery

COMPARISONS notoriously are odious: yet they are part and parcel of life, and have to be recognised. Some people *are* distinctive in accomplishments and attainments; others are "lesser lights"; while the great majority are just ordinary folk—the Smiths and Browns and Robinsons. We meet all ranks and qualities of life in the Bible; and it is fitting that some obscure people should make a brief appearance within its pages. They are, as it were, representatives of the multitude of Christians who, unhonoured and unsung on earth, will yet comprise the great throng around the throne, rejoicing in the Lord eternally, and He in them.

It is characteristic of Paul that he should conclude the profoundest of his epistles with a long series of "pastoral" greetings to those whom he knew among the members of the Church at Rome. To these are added salutations from his companions at Corinth. Together, these present a most fascinating portrait-gallery of the early Church. At the time of writing the epistle, Paul had not visited Rome; but the Imperial city was the magnet which drew travellers from all parts of the world—including members of the Christian Churches which Paul had founded or in which he had ministered. And certain of the Christians of Rome had doubtless, in *their* journeyings abroad, come into contact with the apostle. It is not surprising, therefore, that the list of those known personally to him should be considerable. In these messages to them we are introduced to a representative group of first-century believers, some of whom might be described as the least of the lesser lights (Rom. 16: 1–24).

If these warm-hearted greetings are characteristic of the

apostle, even more so is the fact that he begins with a commendation to the Church at Rome of a visitor from Corinth—who probably was the bearer of the letter: "Phebe our sister, which is a servant—literally 'deaconess'—of the Church which is at Cenchrea." To her the apostle pays this high tribute: "for she hath been a succourer of many, and of myself also." How expressive a phrase that is! A *caring* for the saints is conveyed by the word; a most practical ministry of truly Christian helpfulness. There are different parts to be played in the drama of life; different rôles to fill; different spheres of service for Christ. Paul's was that of the itinerant preacher, enduring much discomfort and weariness—not to speak of persecution and suffering. What a welcome respite it must have been, to receive awhile the considerate attentions of such as Phebe, who would delight to give him the care and comfort he so often lacked during his journeyings. And not only the apostle: she was "a succourer of many"—and therefore worthy to receive succour from the Church at Rome, when herself a traveller and a sojourner in a strange city.

It is thought that Phebe was probably a woman of substance who devoted both her time and possessions to the work of the Lord in Cenchrea—the eastern port of Corinth: so much so that she became the first "deaconess" ministering to her fellow-believers in matters both spiritual and material, and thereby earning enduring renown. Business reasons taking her to Rome, Paul asks the saints there not only to "receive her in the Lord," but also to "assist her in whatsoever business she hath need of you." In all the concerns of life, the Church was expected to foster the welfare of others: to manifest a true brotherliness and practical helpfulness.

Next, Paul greets Priscilla—or Prisca, as she is sometimes called—and Aquila, whom we meet also in the book of Acts (18: 2, 18, 26). Travelling tentmakers like himself, Paul had lodged with them at Corinth; and later they had accompanied him to Ephesus. They had not only shared their home with the apostle, but assisted him in his work for the Lord, and had actually risked their lives in his behalf. That—as our Lord

Himself declared—is the highest sign and seal of friendship. It was, of course, not merely as his friends, but as fellow-labourers in the Gospel that they had thus—to use Paul's graphic phrase —"laid down their own necks" for his sake. What they did was primarily for the Lord, and His Kingdom. The relationship of Christians to one another is determined, first and foremost, by their relationship to the Lord. There is no factor so potent in promoting Christian unity and mutual love, as devotion to the Saviour.

Paul greets also "the Church in their house." Wherever Priscilla and Aquila went, they became the centre of a vital Christian testimony (cf. 1 Cor. 16: 19). They pursued their craft of tentmaking in order to earn their livelihood: but that was incidental to the supreme purpose of their lives—witnessing for Christ. Now returned to Rome, their home had again become the meeting-place of a "local church." And a truly Christian home can be a most effectual testimony. In this, husband and wife were of one mind and will—and from the fact that in four out of the six Scripture references to them the name of Priscilla is placed first, it seems that probably she took the more prominent part of the two. Well, happy is it if the customary order is reversed on occasion, when a wife through superior natural endowments or spiritual zeal takes the lead in Christian service, provided there is full understanding and sympathy between the two. Many a man would be ready to acknowledge how great a debt he owes his wife, not only in loving care and companionship, but also in spiritual example and stimulus. Tragedy creeps in when one or the other lags behind, or even parts company in spiritual conviction and service: but where there is a sharing of faith and vision, what does it matter if the order be "Aquila and Priscilla" or "Priscilla and Aquila"?

No fewer than three members of the Church in Rome, and three of Paul's companions at Corinth, are described by the apostle as his kinsmen. Some commentators suggest that this means "fellow-Jews," since in his discussion of the spiritual state of Israel, in this epistle, he writes of Israelites as "my brethren, my kinsmen according to the flesh" (9: 3, 4). But he obviously

uses the term there metaphorically. He has been writing of the
rejection of the Gospel by Israel, and consequent fulfilment of
the purposes of God in the Gentiles. But he goes on to declare
that his ministry as the apostle to the Gentiles is not accomplished
without heartache for Israel; for is he not a Jew, and are they
not his kinsmen? This strong expression conveys his yearning
that his fellow-Jews should become fellow-believers in Christ.
But to claim that he uses the term in that way in this chapter
also, is to deprive words of their value and language of its
meaning. The comment of Bishop Handley Moule upon the
phrase "my kinsmen" here, is as apposite as it is terse—
"Relatives. Of course in a literal sense, which alone can be
distinctive here."

Two of these kinsmen, says Paul, were "in Christ before me."
What speculation this provokes! Surely he must have known
that Andronicus and Junia were disciples of the despised
Galilean when he was the chief persecutor of the "heretical
sect"? Had their conversion some part in the mental conflict
to which the Lord referred when, in the transforming revelation
on the Damascus road, He chided Paul that it was "hard to
kick against the goad-pricks"? It is customary to attribute his
inward strife to the calm and courageous certainty evinced by
Stephen at his martyrdom. This most probably had a profound
effect upon the young witness of that terrible yet glorious event.
But is it not equally likely that the persuasion of his own kinsmen that Jesus was the Christ, also had shaken him to the
foundations of his being? They could boast equal privileges
of birth and upbringing with himself: and they renounced all
these in becoming disciples of the crucified. That members of
his own family should believe in the Nazarene, inflamed his
anger to such a pitch that he breathed out threatenings and
slaughter against the Christians—and all the while a persistent
voice within raised the query, "Suppose they are right?"

All this is confessedly uncertain, but well within the bounds
of probability. On their part, they would not be surprised at his
bitter antagonism, for our Lord had forewarned His disciples
that they must expect hostility, and most fiercely from members

of their own families. They would, however, certainly pray for their persecutor; and how glad they would be at the wondrous news that "he which persecuted us in times past now preacheth the faith which he once destroyed." Paul describes these two also as his fellow-prisoners—we do not know when or where: he is referring to an imprisonment of which we have no record. Much as we know of his sufferings for Christ's sake, the Bible does not give us the full story, as this allusion indicates. Somewhere, at some time, these kinsmen of his had shared with the apostle an experience of "bonds and imprisonment." And of course they were at all times, like Paul, "captives of Jesus Christ"; they had yielded up their lives to "His grand control." Could one of them have been the nephew who, later, was a means of saving the apostle's life when certain Jews conspired to kill him in Jerusalem (Acts 23: 12–24)? Whether that is so or not, Paul says one thing more of them: that they were "of note among the apostles." This probably means that they were well known to the apostles; but also possibly that they had some distinguished sphere of service in the Church. Worthy kinsmen of Paul indeed!

High in the list—even before his kinsmen—Paul mentions "my well-beloved Epaenetus, who is the firstfruits of Achaia unto Christ." Strangely enough, this is all we know about Epaenetus, yet his conversion, the first in Asia—for so we should read "Achaia"—must have been a thrilling experience to the apostle. We cherish the story of the first convert in Europe, loving to read how Paul addressed the group of devout Jewish women who met every Sabbath beside the river at Philippi to worship Jehovah in simplicity and sincerity of faith, without priest or formal service; and how the Lord opened the heart of Lydia, the seller of purple—and she became the firstfruits in Europe unto Christ. Her counterpart in Asia was Epaenetus. How he had come to believe we do not know, but the few words of Paul's greeting to him glow with lively remembrance and "fatherly" pride and gratitude, in the Lord. However many spiritual "sons" we might be privileged to claim, there is an especial bond of relationship with the "firstborn." No wonder

Paul called him "my beloved"—a term he also applies to others, however, and not distinctive to Epaenetus, as the "wellbeloved" of the A.V. would misleadingly imply.

The bonds of relationship in Christ are indeed strongly expressed in these greetings, and two other brethren, Amplias and Stachys—of whom we know nothing more—are described as "my beloved." As used by the apostle this term possessed, of course, its full wealth of meaning: it signifies nothing less than a deep and true mutual love in Christ. And with a delicacy indicative of profound Christian courtesy, the apostle adapts the phrase from "my beloved" to "the beloved" when he applies it to a woman, Persis, "which laboured much in the Lord." What a model of Christian conduct was the apostle!

Quite a number who, at various times and in differing ways, had either ministered to the apostle or collaborated with him, come briefly before us—"Mary, who bestowed much labour on us"; "Urbane, our helper in Christ"; Tryphena and Tryphosa —probably sisters, and possibly of noble family—"who labour in the Lord"; and "the beloved Persis, which laboured much in the Lord." There seems to be a distinction here, between some who "labour" and others who "labour much." All are appreciated and commended; and all service to and for Christ is assured of its reward: but how great a commendation is due to those who, without reservation or counting the cost, devote their energy and time unstintingly!

A vivid "snapshot" is given of "Apelles, approved in Christ" —and the original is stronger still: "*the* approved . . ." or as Denney paraphrased it, "that approved Christian." In circumstances of which we have no knowledge, Apelles had been put to the test, and proven true and faithful. Groups of slaves in two august households are mentioned—"them which are of Aristobulus' household," and ". . . the household of Narcissus, which are in the Lord." There was a brother of Herod Agrippa named Aristobulus, brought up at Rome in intimate contact with the Imperial family: it is thought that he, on his death, might have bequeathed his slaves to the Emperor, and that these still retained their former designation as "Aristobulus' household": but that is uncertain. It is known that there were Christians in the Imperial palace; but in any event those mentioned were attached to one of the noble families. Their witness in such an environment was like the shining of a star in a dark night.

Two further groups pass in procession before us: "Asyncritus, Phlegon, Hermas, Patrobas, Hermes, and the brethren which are with them" (v. 14); and "Philologus and Julia, Nereus and his sister, and Olympas, and all the saints which are with them" (v. 15). These probably formed little "churches" in the house of the first-named in each instance; for the pattern of early church life was the gathering in the home of one or other member of the local church who could provide a room for the purpose. In Rome there were probably several such groups in different parts of the city, meeting together in larger assemblies when possible, but gathering more frequently in twos and threes or more, for prayer, study of the Scriptures, and mutual encouragement. "Cottage meetings" are as old as the Church!

Finally, a most interesting greeting—to "Rufus, chosen in the Lord, and his mother and mine." Now it is highly probable that this Rufus is the son of Simon of Cyrene, mentioned by Mark in his Gospel as well known among those to whom he was writing (Mark 15: 21). Surely it is one of the most dramatic and moving stories in the whole range of Scripture, that the stranger to Jerusalem who was compelled to carry the cross of Jesus came to learn that, in fact, *the Lord bore that cross for him.* Simon, it would seem, found salvation through faith in the Crucified: and not only he, but his sons also, as Mark reveals. Of course, Rufus was a fairly common name; but the fact that Mark's Gospel was written primarily for the benefit of Roman readers, lends strong support to the belief that the Rufus greeted by Paul was the one to whom Mark refers.

"Chosen in Christ" is how the apostle describes him. All Christians are that, of course; but in some special way Rufus was marked out as "elect"—perhaps for some specific office or service; or as "that choice Christian" (Denney). With him, Paul couples "his mother and mine"—who through an overflowing of "motherly" love and care for the apostle, had established this tender relationship. The most sturdily self-reliant and ruggedly resourceful still need occasional "mothering"; and in this gracious tribute, Paul pays the mother of Rufus the highest compliment which even an apostle could confer.

His personal messages to his friends ended, Paul gives a parting exhortation regarding their relationship with one another, as members of the Church of Christ. "Salute one another," he says, "with an holy kiss" (v. 16). A similar injunction is found in other epistles—1 Corinthians 16: 20 and 2 Corinthians 13: 12; 1 Thessalonians 5: 26; and Peter also uses it, in a slightly different form, "Greet ye one another with a kiss of charity" (1 Pet. 5: 14). A kiss, of course, was the customary mode of salutation, the counterpart in those days of our handshake. We know that this, though usual, was sometimes neglected, as by Simon the Pharisee when he entertained our Lord as his guest (Luke 7: 45). Such neglect was manifestly the display of an intentional superciliousness. It is more than likely, from what we read in the New Testament, that this spirit found its way into some of the Churches. It is rebuked by the apostles, who urge that Christians should exercise courtesy toward one another.

The adjective "holy," however, shows that far more than the customary courtesy is to be observed; this is to be elevated among Christians into a different realm and category. It was not long, however, before the early Church imparted to the word "holy," in this exhortation, the meaning of "ceremonial," and the "ceremonial kiss" was incorporated into the communion service—the men kissing the men, and the women the women. The kiss was, as it were, passed on from one to another, as each in turn kissed his neighbour. This practice continued until the thirteenth century, and still persists in modified form in the Greek Church. Thus have the simplicities of the Gospel, and of the New Testament practice, been perverted.

The true meaning of the word "holy" as used in this connection, is indicated by Peter in his parallel passage—the kiss of charity. The greeting between one Christian and another should be an expression of fellowship in Christ; of love in the Spirit. Christian brotherly love should characterize the gatherings of the Lord's people, and their personal contacts in entering or leaving the place of worship.

The apostles so insistently exhorted the Christians, newly won from heathenism, to greet one another with an holy kiss, because there could be no more powerful incentive to practical godliness, than the heeding of this behest; for if it were obeyed, divisions and strife and envying would of necessity cease. To put it in present-day terms: if Christian people were ever to keep before them the ideal of greeting one another with an holy handshake—a handclasp of brotherly love—those outside would again have reason to exclaim, "How these Christians love one another!"

Even more than this is implied in the exhortation, however. The New Testament applies the term "holy" to those who are, through His wondrous grace, saints—*i.e.* holy ones. We are reckoned holy, in the sight of God, through the redeeming work of our Saviour; and we are exhorted to become so in fact, by the inworking of the Holy Spirit. We are called unto holiness. And where should holiness be more in evidence than in the relationship of His people one with another?

The holy kiss, then, is a greeting between holy ones. They greet one another not merely as fellow men, or even as intimate friends; they kiss—or clasp hands—as those who have passed from death unto life; who acknowledge one Lord; who participate together in one gift of life by the indwelling Holy Spirit. In the ultimate realities of life, the things that matter most, they are at one; they are partners in a great commission, and sharers of a glorious hope. What encouragement, what deepening of Christian love, an holy kiss can impart! It is significant that both the kiss and the handshake are capable of conveying much by way of true spiritual fellowship: and both can be perverted into its very antithesis. Judas betrayed his Lord and ours with a kiss. So, often, do we.

So an holy kiss must be the expression of an holy life. An unholy man cannot impart an holy kiss. An holy kiss cannot accompany unholy thoughts—and unkind, supercilious, impatient thoughts, toward a brother in Christ, are unholy. An holy kiss is the pledge and token of the supreme human relationship, transcending sex and race and age and disposition, and every other factor: that those who love the Lord are "all one in Christ Jesus."

The galaxy of saints presented to us in this remarkable chapter is completed in the salutations of Paul's companions at Corinth, who join him in Christian good wishes to their fellow-believers at Rome—and thereby provide us with a further short series of thumb-nail sketches. Timothy, the apostle's "fellow-labourer", comes first; his dearest companion and devoted "son" in the faith. His three kinsmen, Lucius, Jason and Sosipater; and "I Tertius, who wrote this epistle"—Paul's amanuensis, who wished his readers to know that the penman was no mere scribe, but a brother in Christ. Here is a sentence in a Pauline epistle which Paul did not dictate! There is a delightful informality in the laconic phrase, "Gaius mine host, and of the whole church, saluteth you." Paul had earlier encouraged the Roman Christians to be "given to hospitality" (12: 13), and here he presents an example of it, in Gaius, who not only entertained the apostle, but kept "open house" for "the whole church."

One of the comparatively few early Christians of exalted position receives only the same passing mention as humble believers—"Erastus, the chamberlain (treasurer) of the city, saluteth you," and last of all, "Quartus, a brother." It is eminently fitting that this kaleidoscope of first-century saints should terminate with one of whom we know nothing more than that he was "a brother in Christ." What kind of man he was, what gifts he possessed, what station he occupied: these all, upon which the world sets such store, fade into oblivion in the onward march of the centuries; but the fact of relationship *to* and *in* Christ, is of abiding verity. If any man is "in Christ," he is a new creation—a son of God and heir of eternal blessedness; if he is truly "a brother" he fulfils life's richest responsibilities.

These glimpses of the folk who made up representative assemblies of the early Church bring to us anew the apostolic standard of values. Social distinctions disappear—or should do —in the fellowship of saints; and spiritual relationship and service are seen to be the things of abiding worth. Few can aspire to a place among those whom the world calls great or the Church esteems as its prophets and seers: but the "lesser lights" have inestimable privilege and unbounded possibilities—and an assured place among the most exalted of the sons of men, when the Lord shall gather His saints, to be with Him for ever.